7 STEPS
TO
CLARITY

How to use your personal guidance system to live your best life

NICOLE STEPHEN, PhD

7 Steps to Clarity: How to use your personal guidance system to live your best life by Nicole Stephen
Published 2019 by Your Book Angel
Copyright © Nicole Stephen

Printed in the United States
Edited by Keidi Keating
Layout by Rochelle Mensidor

ISBN: 978-1-7341814-4-9

TABLE OF CONTENTS

INTRODUCTION

Do you ever wonder what your life is all about? Why you are here? You are not alone. As a coach and teacher for many years, there is a common thread that runs through students, young professionals, and even CEOs at the height of their careers: "So what? Now what?" And there is confusion, lots of confusion. "Do I stay in my current job? How can I get a better job? Do I start a family? Do I stay with my current spouse? Why haven't I found love yet? Why didn't I stay in the band? I would have had such a different life. Maybe I should be doing something more important, something worthy to impact the world in a positive and meaningful way?"

What if I told you that there is a guru—a genie perhaps—that can answer all your questions? This person can make themselves available to you day or night, can answer any question, and can give you clear insights on any situation or decision, no matter how small or difficult. And this guru is free of charge and full of love and support for you. Too good to be true? Well, it is true and the person who has all the answers to unlock your potential with ease and fun is, yes, you may have guessed it, YOU!

In this book, I am going to give you 7 simple steps to find your way back to yourself and to your highest guidance, which is your God-given birthright, which unfortunately has been taken away from you because of our culture, upbringing, and conditioning. A large majority of people have lost their way, but you will now confidently walk your path with purpose and passion. This is not to say that you will never be confused again, but if you tap into the powers that exist within yourself—and I will do my best to show you how—you will experience a completely different reality than you have to date.

7 Steps to Clarity is a path, a way, a journey for you to undertake with yourself and for yourself. No one can do this with you or for you. There is no more important journey. Yes, of course people can help you along the way, but in the end you must choose, again and again, to put yourself first and to find the answers that only you seek and that only you have. Peace and happiness are what most people are after in their lives. The myriad of ways that we find to achieve these things is what makes us all appear to be so different. But at our core, this is what most of us are after— peace and happiness for ourselves and peace and happiness for our loved ones.

This book is about coming home to yourself, to the YOU that you were born as before other people and the world started telling you what to believe. This book is about cleaning up your life so that you can be a beacon of hope for others and serve the world in the ways that only you can. This is my intention for you and for this book: that it lead you in the direction of your clarity and that you find greater peace, happiness, love, and adventure in your life as a result of it.

Each chapter includes the following:

- Quotes that represent the key concepts in the chapter
- A summary of what the step is and how it can benefit you
- A few examples for you to consider/stories of application
- Signs you are moving in the right direction
- Questions to consider for your life

To get the most from this book you will want to engage with the content in more than just a surface way, especially the questions at the end of each chapter. How you do that can vary greatly but one recommendation likely to work well is getting a new journal or a blank notebook that you can use to write notes and reflections throughout the book as well as to jot down your answers to the questions at the end of each chapter. Ideally, you would even use these questions to engage with a trusted friend or small group, allowing you all go deeper in your pursuit of growth and clarity. While the book is laid out in 7 steps, in reality the growth process is anything but linear so feel free to skip around in the questions in whatever way work best for you. Listen to your own intuition around where it makes sense to go deeper. After you have read through the book once, you may want to use it as a reference when certain steps become more relevant for your life. No matter how you choose to engage with the questions, take this rare opportunity to reflect and know that these questions are simply a jumping off point for the questions you will continue to ask yourself in service of your ever-increasing clarity and to guide you to your best future.

STEP 1
AWARENESS

"We are not human beings having a spiritual experience. We are spiritual beings having a human experience."

Pierre Teilhard de Chardin

"You are gods, sons of the Most High, all of you."

Jesus

You have so much more potential than you realize. You are not your body. You are not the roles you play. You are not the jobs you hold. You are a soul having a human experience and you always have access to higher guidance. You do not have to believe this for it to be true. But you do need to find a way to understand this at a deep enough level, in order to accept the magnificent implications of it. Your soul is an individuation of God. You are a part of God and God is part of you. Because of this, you have access to your higher potential in each moment. Now some people prefer not to think of God and so it is equally appropriate to think of your connection to Source, to the Universe, Life, or even your Highest Self. It matters not what your belief system is. If you are focused on the brain, then know that the brain is like a muscle that will continue to grow and get stronger as it is exercised. If you are focused on the body, know that you have only barely begun to see what your body—made up of 11 interdependent systems—is capable of. If you are focused on your senses, know that the 5 senses you use on a daily basis are just the tip of the iceberg for what is available to us—most of us know about our unrealized 6th sense, but the more likely number is 9, and some people believe there are upwards of 20 senses! Are you consciously tapping into all these potentials each day? I know I am not, but how amazing if we started to move in that direction. By expanding your view of what is possible, you will invite opportunity to use new ways of thinking and being which will create a virtuous cycle. Unfortunately, for many of us, we create a vicious cycle by using less and less of our minds, bodies, and senses, and drawing the square around us so small that we barely believe we can get through the day. This sense of limitedness is not how we are meant to live.

Awareness means that we understand we can tap into these greater potentials at any given time. In other words, there is no moment in your entire life that is more holy or more important than any other. I remember the first time I heard this truism and it immediately struck me as having profound implications. You mean to tell me that when I am playing with my kids or having an important conversation with my best friend, these moments have the same holiness, the same potential, the same opportunity as when I am at the office doing a mundane task? Or when I am fighting with my husband? Can't be! But it is true. You are always connected to God, you are always holy, and each moment is as equally filled with potential as the next. Wow! Once you grasp that, you start to understand how it is that you always, in all moments, and in all ways, have access to your highest guidance.

Awareness also means that you know you are at cause in your own life. If we are at cause in our lives, and I believe we are, then we must become more aware of our intentions, drivers, thoughts, feelings, and words. The more attuned we can become to what is driving us to do something, the thoughts that continue to pass through us, and our emotions—especially the ones simmering below the surface—the more we are in a place to change or release these things. Stuffing, ignoring, or generally refusing to look at ourselves in this way is a surefire way to get stuck and to continue to make the same mistakes over and over again. You are much more powerful than you know, and your intentions matter more than most people realize which is why it is beneficial to become aware, really aware of what you are choosing and WHY! Once we understand our deeper motivations and intentions, we can consider if these are the intentions we wish to act on or not. Most of the time we are careless, casual, and reactive in our intentions, our thoughts and our words and therefore we don't always recognize the outcomes we are driving.

Why do you do what you do? Why are you waking up and going to that job each day? Why do you love how you feel when you are swimming? Why are you driving all over town to get your kids to sports on time? Why are you watching 3 hours of TV each night while drinking 3 glasses of wine? Start asking these questions of yourself and allow yourself to discover the answers. In my experience, most of us have fallen into our lives and many of our choices by happenstance. We are doing it because someone told us it was the appropriate thing to do or because we have formed a habit, but we have not really reflected on its meaning for us. Now, I know what some of you are thinking: This could be paralyzing. But this need not be the case. We do not have to have a significant meaningful reason for each thing we do each day; however, I would argue that if we don't at least start to reflect on what it is we are doing and being, then our lives can 'get away from us' in a way and we can one day 'wake up' and wonder how we got here. For example, before I started my own company, I was working for a mid-size corporation that made fun and entertaining products and yet when I started to question why I was in this job, the answers were eye-opening. I was making good money and had a great team, but I asked myself, "How would you spend your time and what contribution would you make if you already had all the money you needed?" This question took me down a path of really identifying the most important contributions that I want to make in this lifetime and in the end, I was able to make a better decision for myself.

Intentions and Impact.

The concept of Intentions and Impact is core to the coaching work I do with individuals and teams. The most relevant takeaways worth sharing are that our intentions do not always equal the impact felt by others and that most people have little awareness of their intentions and definitely are not aware of their 'deeper' intentions. Once we are able to really ask ourselves the question of why we are doing something and what our true intentions are, that alone can help shift us because sometimes we quickly (or not so quickly) realize that the truth behind the intention is being driven by something outside of ourselves—society, parental expectations, habit—and is not being thoughtfully identified. It is still true that you can have extremely positive intentions and the impact on others may be felt in a less than positive way, but in my experience, the more you 'clean up' your intentions, the less likely you are to have an impact that is different than you intended. But if you are operating at a surface level awareness (e.g., "Well, I gave her that feedback about her communication style being annoying because we are supposed to give each other feedback"), then it will often be the case that you are surprised by the negative impact that your thoughts and words have on others.

Let's say we get up and go running every morning, 7 days a week. We do this when we are tired and when we don't feel well and then we are proud of ourselves that we are so disciplined. If we get in touch with our intention for running by asking the question, we may find out that one aspect of our motivation is that we are fearful of what will happen if we don't do this. In this example, let's say we each had a parent that died early from heart disease and at some level, we believe that we must make our hearts as strong and healthy as possible. Is this a bad thing? Good thing? The truth is that there is no good or bad here. But if we overlay onto our example that we hate running and we resent the time we spend doing this, what do you think now? What if we were to refine our intention to find something we could do that would make us healthy and we would enjoy? With that intention, we might allow ourselves to run 5 days a week. Or perhaps we would find that we actually love yoga and we are happy to do that 7 days a week. Someone else who runs 7 days a week may be doing this because they want to be healthy and they love how running makes them feel. In this case, we would all say that their intention is working for them. But in the first example, the intention is not fully working and thus, it is more likely we will not achieve our desired outcomes. Do you see the nuance? As we get clearer about our intentions, we will continue to refine our decisions and actions so that they are all working for us and with us!

So why does staying aware or raising our level of awareness matter? It matters because if you are so much more than what you think you are, you must allow yourself to experience this in your reality. You can only know yourself to the extent that you allow yourself to. Now don't panic, because the good news is that you will continue to grow through your experiences no matter what you choose now and there will eventually come a day when you recognize that you were never 'just' your body or the limitations you believe you have, but you can have access to greater and greater experiences to the extent you allow yourself to realize it now. So, why wait?! Your physical body is an out-picturing of your energetic body. Your thoughts, emotions, words, food all have energy that affects your connection to your highest guidance. Understand that you are not alone and there is so much more potential in this moment, in this instant, than you are allowing. Know this deeply and it alone can change your life. Again, you are at cause in your own life; you have power, great power and you need to find ways to harness it for good—your own good and the good of others. You need not live a dreary, sad difficult existence. Being aware will not stop the challenges from coming but it will empower you to move through them with greater ease and grace.

If you really were aware that TODAY is your teacher, all of the day—the emails, the phone calls, the random people you meet on the street, your stream of thoughts, the laundry that waits for you—how would you approach it differently? Would you slow down and look around more? Would you take time to reflect before you speak and before you act? Might you even have a little more fun with it, realizing that the energy you put into it is exactly the energy you will receive back? It is quite a wondrous concept really and we would be well served to learn the truth of this before it is too late. We are our own best teachers and our higher selves are trying hard to lead us to our 'perfect' paths which will in almost all cases look different than our ego-driven 'small' self thinks they should. But remember, different does not need to be worse, and it certainly can be better if we are aware enough to release our expectations of who we are and what we can become. So, find ways to clear up the line to your greater potential. Sometimes the line is clear and at other times there is a lot of static. And sometimes, even though the line is open, we have put earphones on and are listening to something completely different. So, in order to find your clarity, it is important to open the lines of communication in whatever ways work for you.

"How do I stay aware?" you may ask, and this is an important question. There are many ways to remember and to stay in awareness. It really depends on you. The most important thing to note is that there is nothing you need to *do* to remember. This is not about taking action. I could write an entire list of things for you to do each day when you wake up and while some of them may be helpful, it would put you out of your own knowing and you would start to believe in the actions or the behaviors, instead of believing in yourself. So, the advice is this. Each morning when you wake up out of bed, remind yourself: "I am not this body; I am one with God and God is one with me. I am in constant communication with my Source, with my Highest Self and therefore I am safe, loved, and guided. So be it." Simple and straightforward. If it feels hard, it is only because you are stuck in patterns that you have created over a lifetime and while they feel immovable, they are not. There is so much more potential for each of us, completely untouched and below our level of consciousness, that we have the power to tap into—in each instant, in each day.

To become more aware, we must take the time needed to reflect on who we are and why we are here. We live in a world filled with distraction, so much so that you could easily live a life today without a single moment of silent introspection if you did not cultivate this for yourself. This is not sustainable and we each must find our own way to the silence within. Until we make it a priority, it will never just happen. The good news is that it won't take a lot of time, once you start to prioritize yourself. You will see benefits and making the time will get easier and easier. But you must start where you are. Most of us won't get to a threshold level of awareness if we aren't able to take time out of the day to reflect on this. Thus, the environment we have created—where there are thousands, even millions of distractions available at each moment with the advent of the internet and accessible media content—means that we must consciously choose to spend time with ourselves as it is unlikely to just 'happen' that we are alone and quiet with nothing to do.

Being in nature is a great way to expand our awareness as can be religion, spiritual books or inspiration, music, yoga, qi gong, or many other practices that enhance our focus on energy and potential. Some people enjoy going to the spa or on retreats and these can also help us enhance our perspective if we allow them to. The point is not that there is something you must do, but rather that you must allow your awareness to expand beyond where it has been before. Often times, it takes a serious challenge—whether it be grief or illness or difficult relationships—to force us into some solo time of reflection that leads to a greater awareness of who we are and why we are here, and yet it need not take these difficult situations if we allow the time and energy needed as some kind of regular practice, whether it be sitting in silent meditation, listening to music, writing, walking in nature, gardening, etc. It is true that awareness of our larger potential comes and goes—that is part of the human experience—but remembering and reminding yourself of this truth *often* is the key. There will come a time when you just know, when you no longer need to remember, but until then, you would do well to find ways to remind yourself.

Try being more mindful for one day. Mindfulness just means being fully aware in this moment. Sounds simple, but have you tried it? I am constantly involved in many different things and being fully in my body, in my experience in this moment, is a continuing journey for me. Yet, the only place we really live is in the present. There are many great books on this topic that you can read but my main point is this: The more you can tune in and turn up your senses—all of them, in each moment—the more this new level of awareness will surprise you in terms of both how much there is to experience and the residual positive effects it creates in your life. For example, I know of people who stopped over-eating and as a result, lost weight they had been 'struggling with' for years by being more mindful while eating. Sounds simplistic— well, it is simple—but it is not always easy for those of us who have been conditioned to numb ourselves to avoid dealing with our feelings in the present moment.

Religious, Spiritual, Both, or Neither?

In my coaching, I never ask people about their religious affiliation and it rarely comes up in this context. However, I am well aware that the way we are raised, if we are affiliated with a certain religion, our current beliefs about God, Life, Universe, who we are and what we are doing here have major implications for our motivations and our abilities to gain clarity and to accelerate our growth. At its most fundamental, religion is defined as: *a set of beliefs concerning the cause, nature, and purpose of the universe, especially when considered as the creation of a superhuman agency or agencies, usually involving devotional and ritual observances, and often containing a moral code governing the conduct of human affairs.* Thus, to the extent that religion helps us connect to our roles in the universe, teaches us how to contact a higher power, helps us understand ways of behaving that serve us and serve humanity, and lifts us beyond the material world, it can benefit us greatly. However, as most now understand, religion can also become—whether intentionally or unintentionally—a way to pigeonhole people into a set of beliefs that separate people from themselves, from each other, and from their own experiences of God and Life. Because of this, many people's experiences with religion have not been positive and it is why so many people speak of 'being spiritual,' yet not religious. Regardless of your religious affiliation, your perception of your own spirituality and belief or non-belief in a higher power, cultivating awareness that we are more than the current state of our physical bodies and that we have much greater potential is beneficial.

To raise your awareness in some ways is the same thing as raising your consciousness, which is also related to raising your energy. Therefore, we can actively raise our levels of energy and consciousness which will have the by-product of raising our awareness. Effective ways to do this include yoga and meditation. These are ancient traditions and science is just now beginning to understand the powerful, positive effects they have on the mind and body. If this is appealing to you, there are thousands of books, recordings, and classes to get you started. But know that each minute spent going inward—in whatever approach you take—is worth its weight in gold and will pay dividends. Even if you are starting from nothing, 2 minutes, then 5 minutes a day, and then 2 minutes and 5 minutes an hour will do wonders for your relaxation and ironically also increase your energy and awareness. People spend thousands, sometimes millions of dollars trying to find this energy outside themselves with things like fancy cars or houses or vacations and what is really needed is a way to shut out the world in way that is not shutting ourselves down (like alcohol, drugs, or sleep does to us), but shutting out the world and raising ourselves up.

Your life proceeds out of your intention for it. So, if you are intent on realizing your potential and you know, capital-K Know, that there is much more to who you are a deeper level, you will allow your life to reflect this. That is all that is required. It is simple, but you must be open to this truth for you to see the benefits. If I can tap into greater knowing at any time, does that mean it's possible to know things before they happen? Sure, it is possible; we have all had this experience, yet many of us don't pay enough attention and therefore the power of the intuition or knowing is limited. As you walk on this journey of reclaiming YOU, of trusting yourself, you will learn to pay much closer attention to what you do know, and you will begin to act on this knowing.

Knowing that Defies a 5-Senses Explanation.

When my husband's father died, I had an experience of knowing that defies any 5-senses explanation. It was supposed to be our second date and he did not call and did not show up. I was disappointed as we had been out on one previous afternoon date and had a great time. That night, I had a vivid dream that he called me and as I picked up the phone, I knew it was him. I knew it was him but all I could hear was choked back crying. He could not speak. Without words, in my dream, he told me that his father had died and that he would come to me when he could. The next morning, I woke up and called a friend to share a description of my dream. I learned 2 weeks later when he did call that his father had passed away the same night as my dream. Interestingly, he had not even shared with me that his father was sick when we went out. But even if one could think of it as a strange coincidence, the level of knowing that I experienced was complete, meaning I knew what I knew completely and there are not really words to describe this. I have had this happen a few other times. One time when I was headed down a path with a man that was never meant to be, and despite my strong desire that things would work out, I had a series of dreams, filled with the knowledge that it was not meant to be. It took me a while to accept this even though in this instance the knowledge was also complete.

This is not about you having special powers or being more special than others. This awareness I write about is true of *all* of us. Thus, it has major implications for how we think about and treat one another—which we will talk more about in the chapter on responsibility. This awareness also means believing that the Source of all your blessings is God or the Universe or your Highest Self. These blessings include things as practical as your income, your food, and your place to live. Thus, these are areas of your life you need to go to your highest wisdom on. Far too often we leave these areas unexamined because someone, somewhere told us how things ought to be and we believed them. What would it mean for you if you KNEW that the source of all your blessings was God, the Universe, your Highest Self? What would it mean for how you think and talk about your career, your income, your responsibilities? This is a foreign concept to most of us because we have been raised to believe that we must work for everything, that we are on a scarce planet with scarce resources and that only the good, only the hard-working, only the chosen ones get to live their best lives. What if this teaching is all wrong? If we go back to all the spiritual teachings, they each tell us that God is the giver of the gifts, that it is only our mindset of scarcity that makes our reality of scarcity true. But what of the situation on the planet now where many people do not have enough to eat, where many people do not have homes, or are living in poverty? Isn't this scarcity real in our current reality? The lesson here is one of unity and belief that there is enough for all. There, of course, is enough for all if we learn the lesson of sharing with others; however, this does not mean that we need to give away all that we own. It does mean that we must become aware of our abundance and as we become aware of it, we will share it, and as we share it, it will expand and it is in this expansion that we will finally realize that we were creating the scarcity after all.

There will be signs when you begin living your life from a place of greater awareness. First, you will notice more—more details, more depth, more possibilities than ever before. You will also be more grateful; you will notice how life does support you and not passively, but actively. You will enjoy your life more; you will be more interested and engaged in what is happening because finally you realize that there is a larger purpose at play—that you are part of a larger tapestry at work and it is truly fascinating as you become aware of the interconnectedness of your life with so many others. You will stop being so caught up in your mini dramas, in the nuances of how others treat you, or how others are living their lives. You will be too busy paying attention to your own. You have the potential to become more loving. Awareness in and of itself will not make you loving; however, as you start to become aware of the major principles at work in the universe—that what you send out is returned to you, for example—you may be more inclined to lead with compassion than in the past. Love, joy, and happiness ultimately are what you will allow to flow through you when you are completely at peace with who and what you are. This peace is always available to you at any time.

As you ask the questions below, use them as ways to awaken your awareness and then once awakened, as tools to help direct the flow of your life.

QUESTIONS TO CONSIDER:

- Who do you really think you are? Why are you here? Seriously spend time pondering this question.
- Who would you be without your body? What role does your body play for you? Is it how you define yourself? Is it the out-picturing of your inner state? Is it a communication device for your soul? Coming to deeper conclusions about your body is critical to ensuring that you don't spend your entire life focused on the surface level. If you knew you would live long after this body is gone, what difference would it make in your perspective? In your life?
- What roles, thoughts, behaviors, experiences from your past do you believe define you? What would happen if you were to release these or loosen these as no longer defining? Who are you without those roles or experiences, without your stories, your accomplishments, your failures, your name, your country, etc.? For many this is a scary thought, but stay with it, and let the answer reveal itself to you.
- What are the ways that you can gain a greater perspective? E.g., exercise, meditation, prayer, church, being in nature. Find time to sit with this larger perspective and see what it can do for you.
- What would your eternal self or your most authentic YOU care about that you haven't been spending much time or energy on? How can you integrate more of this into your life?

STEP 2
HONESTY

"...and ye shall know the truth, and the truth shall set you free."

John 8:32

"Honesty is the first chapter in the book of wisdom."

Thomas Jefferson

Lies, lies and more lies. Our society has gone so far into lies that there is confusion about what is true. So, step 2 is to clean up your own house. Stop worrying about what is on the TV or the newspaper or your social media site. Forget about all the lies from the politicians, the celebrities, your friends and family and focus on yourself. Are you being honest with yourself? Really honest with yourself? Allow yourself to see clearly what is working and not working in your life. You will come to see that there are many ways we lie to ourselves each day. These lies are shown in the world at large, but again, the way back to yourself is through yourself and yourself only. So, what are you lying about? Is it your hair color? Is it your desire to be helpful to your friends? Is it your engagement with your job? Is it your feelings toward your spouse? Is it the clothes you are wearing? The bags you are buying? The food you are eating? The prayers you are asking? Now this may seem confusing at first. But ask yourself the question. How am I lying to myself about these things? Take a minute and write down the answers or just sit with the answers. They will come. There will be big and small things. Do not let this overwhelm you. This is productive. Let the lies surface. Do not be ashamed or fearful. Such is true for all of us. When the lies surface, acknowledge them, bless them, and then ask your Higher Self for the way forward. It does not mean you need to be running outside and shouting your new truth from the rooftops. Although it could be, it is more likely that a way will be shown to you to slowly and deliberately acknowledge your own truth in each area of your life. These small steps will open the way to living the life of clarity that you desire.

What about the lies of others? What of that honesty? As you clarify your own lies, you will absolutely begin to see the ways that others are lying to themselves and yes, sometimes to you. Resist the urge to point this out to them. This is your journey and the best way for you to lead others is to live your truth. Put down your weapons and tell your truth—quietly and confidently—and this will light the way for others. When you are in judgement of others, even of their lies, you are not in your own truth. Everyone lies—to themselves and others—and part of the journey is to acknowledge and move away from this. You are responsible for doing this for yourself so that you may show the way to others. You are absolutely not asked to point out the lies of others unless you are personally called to do so, which we will address later. Do not make yourself the truth cop. You are seeing things differently now. You will see the lies and acknowledge them. They will then be replaced for you with truths. Small truths at first and then big truths—truths of your Higher Self. Accept these, be grateful for them, and let them lead you.

The truth shall set you free. As your truth awakens, let it guide you to the next shore. You do not realize the weight that your lies have laid on you, so with each one that you look at directly, let the light take over it. You will feel a lightness that you have never known. This is the reason why when people 'come out of the closet' or finally reveal a truth that they have been holding, they are often transformed into who they were always meant to be. The shame and judgement that you foresee coming to you as a result of speaking your truth may come or it may not, but in either case, so be it. You will be OK. In fact, by telling your truth you will be more than OK, and you will light a way for others.

Lying Can Make You Sick.

I have many examples of this phenomenon from friends and those I have coached and I have even experienced it myself. You tell a 'white lie'. For example, you answer a plea for help with "I can't fill in for you at work tomorrow as I am not feeling well," or "We can't go out that night because one of the kids is sick," only to have yourself or your child become ill in the way that you had described to others. I have learned this lesson and hope not to repeat it. Yet, I think there are subtler ways that we lie to ourselves and others that we don't acknowledge and that may then influence our well-being and our health. Many therapist friends have shared stories with me of health symptoms that have been reversed in their patients when they were able to confront an area of life where they were not in integrity. I myself had an experience where I was in denial of my own lack of loyalty and I continued to get an upset stomach until I finally realized the association and came clean both in my actions and in my willingness to take responsibility for my actions.

I often have people ask me about how telling the truth influences the lives of children. We spend a lot of time encouraging our kids to tell white lies, good lies, lies that won't hurt others. "Tell Grandma she is beautiful." "Tell them you like the shirt they gave you." "Tell the man you are 5 years old instead of 7 so we can get the discount." You will decide for yourself how to handle this with your kids; there is no one right answer. But do know they are watching you and paying close attention. Teaching children manners and more importantly, compassion for others and to look beneath the surface (e.g., Grandma really is beautiful even though you keep noticing her wrinkling skin and her sad face) will serve them very well. Teaching them to lie so that they may get something they want or to influence others to a behavior that is in their self-interest is perhaps not the highest teaching for children who will then need to unlearn these habits later in life in order to have honest dialogue with others.

If I am lying to myself, how will I know? You already know on some level. So, the idea is to allow yourself to see it, let it float up to consciousness. It is OK, there is nothing there to fear, just habits and lies, and misconceptions you have held about yourself and others that are all ready to be released. Just see it, let it go, and watch it be replaced. It really is that easy!

For example, for years I thought and told people that I was not energetic, not sporty, and hated running. At some point I realized that this belief came from a story my parents shared about me when I was 3 about getting spinal meningitis and having to relearn to walk and talk, and never really having the same level of energy again. I had somehow internalized this story, which was repeated often in my home, and thus my experience was that I was not sporty or energetic and I hated running. When I turned 30, I was going through a challenging time and I decided that I would run a marathon. I faced this story about myself as 'just a story' and I set out to run 26 miles with a download of a program off the internet and a vision of crossing the finish line. Three months and 48 runs under my belt, I finished the marathon with a slow, but respectable time and forever changed my self-perception of what I was capable of. Perhaps another example is in order, lest you believe that you must go out and run a marathon which is not the point of the story. It took me many years to realize that some of the negative stories I was telling myself about my husband—that he was selfish, that he didn't love me enough—were really about me. I was the one behaving selfishly and when I really looked at it, I was certainly not acting lovingly toward him. This was a tough truth for me to swallow. But when I let it come to the surface, the revelation slowly started to change how I saw our dynamics. Now, in this case it was not changed overnight. It took me many years (and still can be a challenge now) for me to come to a place where I can see the relationship, and my role in it, clearly. This clarity has opened the way for a significant shift and more love in our relationship. It's less about active behavior change, and much more a shift in understanding and compassion for him. This is a good example, because along with the realization of how I was influencing the relationship in a negative way could have come shame and regret which could easily have overtaken everything else if I had let it. Thanks to my willingness to forgive—myself and him—and thanks to God's willingness to let me heal, I was able to see my destructive role and move forward with positivity and grace and even a little bit of patience for myself when I revert back to my old blaming patterns.

Carrying lies, speaking lies, living lies takes an extraordinary amount of energy. As you begin to allow yourself to see the truth, you will fill up with so much energy and joy that you didn't even realize you had. Allowing yourself to see the areas where you have not had integrity is important because it is only once you allow these to be seen that they can be corrected for you. One of the beautiful things to know is that the surfacing of the lies need not cause shame or even dishearten you, but rather as they are seen, so shall they be lifted. It is in the lifting that you will feel lighter and happier and allow yourself to feel more joy. So, don't be afraid of the lies—again, we all have them—but allow yourself to see the areas you have not been living your values or your truth.

What Are My Values?

I volunteer teach at our county jail in a 10-week class sponsored by a local non-profit focused on conflict transformation and anger management for inmates who will soon be released back into the community. One of the focus areas is about values so we talk about what values are, what values people hold dear, and the potential for conflict when people hold different values. When we do this class, it is always a lively one as people are passionate about their values and can easily see how value clashes lead to conflict. But what has also been eye-opening for me is the reaction—in both the men and women's classes—that some have forgotten about their values or they have simply stopped spending any time considering them or perhaps they never thought of their values in a conscious way before. They appreciate seeing a long list of values because it reminds them that they in fact were taught certain values and even now hold values dear and yet none of this is conscious. Once conscious, it is helpful because then we can assess when we are living our lives consistently with our values and when we are not. It is also interesting to note how quickly the participants recognize that even for the values they hold dear (e.g., freedom, love, fairness), their behaviors do not always support these values. I have taught similar classes with executives and interestingly, the reaction is quite similar!

One of the ways we lie to ourselves is by ignoring areas of our lives that we know need attention, but we choose to avoid looking at them directly. Our finances, our health, and our relationships are areas where we often choose to look away instead of taking stock of the current state of things. When we finally do look with clarity, it may be extremely difficult to see the messes we have made and yet, it is the unwillingness to look at them directly that holds them firmly in place. Once we muster the courage to open our eyes to these areas that are desperately trying to get our attention, we will have access to many ways to improve the situation.

A Marriage Full of Lies.

A client of mine found out that his wife had been cheating on him over a period of many years. This turned out to be one of the smallest lies he would encounter as he ended his marriage of 25 years. I wish I could say that the breakup was the wake-up call she needed to start living a life with integrity; however, even after months of therapy and the marriage officially ended, the lies continued. My client went to therapy himself to try to process everything that happened; the experience of uncovering all the lies made him wonder if their entire life was a lie. As he questioned the entire marriage and his role in it, he did come to realize that there were signs and flags along the way that he chose to ignore. Little voices in his head that he pushed away, knowing he was being lied to, but choosing to ignore because it was easier until it wasn't.

While this is an extreme example, stories like this one abound in our own lives and in the lives of our friends and colleagues. We don't have to look too far to see a version of ourselves in the story. Perhaps we haven't cheated on a spouse, but maybe we have crossed a line or two at times. Perhaps we occasionally tell a white lie to our friends or clients when it is in our best interest. To drive clarity in our own lives, we need to stop judging others for their mistakes, and we need to be willing to see and accept the lies—firstly, our own and then those of our loved ones. Otherwise, we live a surface-level, inauthentic and low-integrity life that will not propel us in the direction of clarity of purpose for our lives.

You will know you are moving in the right direction when you catch yourself exaggerating or telling white lies and are able to stop yourself before you do or clarify the truth as soon as you realize it. You will feel lighter and less concerned with interactions because you no longer have anything to hide or a certain impression you need to leave on others. You will trust yourself more; you are trustworthy and that means something. For some of us, this step to clarity is an important yet relatively not difficult one. For others, releasing the need to lie is a life's work but it need not take a lifetime to do it. Allow yourself to let the lies go, just watch them bubble up and away.

QUESTIONS TO CONSIDER:

- What are the small and big ways you lie to yourself? Why?
- What are the small and big ways you lie to others? Why?
- What do you know to be 'true for you'? Write down your top 10 truths. It matters not at all whether you share these with others. It matters 100% that you live them.
- Examine one lie closely. What is it? Where did it come from? What purpose does it serve? What energy (if any) would be freed up if you were to release the lie entirely?
- Is it possible, step by step, to start becoming more honest with yourself and others? If so, where is a good place to start?

STEP 3
RESPONSIBILITY

"When you think everything is someone else's fault, you suffer a lot. When you realize everything springs only from yourself, you will learn both peace and joy."

Dalai Lama

"Have only love in your heart for others. The more you see the good in them, the more you will establish the good in yourself."

Paramahansa Yogananda

Responsibility is about taking full responsibility for your own life and about taking some level of responsibility for the people, events, and interactions that surround you. Trouble. Injury. Illness. Accidents. War. They are all the same, they are the out-picturing of our internal states. I am not speaking here of 'blaming the victim'. Rather, asking people to take responsibility for themselves is the most empowering thing we can do for ourselves and for each other. We don't know our own power and yet we all have it, every one of us. *Everything* that shows up in your life is an opportunity—an opportunity to grow, an opportunity to heal, an opportunity to love—if seen as one. If not, it becomes an obstacle—at least temporarily.

There is much sadness in the world today and there need not be. Depression, suicides, gun violence are all on the rise. These are symptoms of a disconnected world that has forgotten its connection to a higher source and to each other. Blame is not needed to turn this trend around, yet a clear and unflinching look at the current state of affairs is. The world around us—from the family that shows up at your kitchen table, to the view from your bedroom window, to what shows up on the nightly news— is the environment we find ourselves in and therefore it is this environment that we must accept and then work to change if we are not happy with what we are encountering. Where we get lost is that we believe we must have control over it in order to change it or else we must just ignore it. Yet, there are many ways that we each can exert a positive influence on our environments. It is always about our mindsets and our behaviors—never just one. So, if we are not sure what actions we can take, then it is best to search our minds to see if the way we are viewing a situation is contributing to the challenges that are occurring. Once we can shift our mindsets, even just a little, we have access to many more favorable actions. Unfortunately, many of us have been raised to believe that we need to change the mindsets of others instead of ourselves, which is a downward spiral that will never create the change we are looking for. It is our job to reflect on our own minds, our own perspectives, our own actions and to make changes here. By doing this, we will be led, step by step to opportunities to increase our influence with others.

What does it mean to be a grown up? It means taking responsibility for your life. It means that each of us must take 100% responsibility for our mindsets and our actions. To the extent that we find people to blame—politicians, neighbors, spouses, kids—is the extent to which we still need to grow up. As I write this, I am quite clear that I am not there yet either, and yet I know that this is the way to freedom from the tyranny of believing that we can and should control others' views and behaviors and all the while ignore what is not yet clear about our own perspectives and actions.

Taking responsibility for your life does not mean that you are always serious, have no fun, and live a life of only obligations. Taking responsibility in some ways means freedom from others' imposed obligations until and unless you have decided that these are choices you wish to make. Becoming an adult, becoming responsible sounds like it is boring and limiting and it is in this that we have it all wrong. True responsibility means that you are the one in charge of your own life and while you may still choose to do things with and for others—and I encourage you to do so— you also may choose to do many things that others don't approve of or don't understand because they are areas of interest or passion for you. Taking responsibility for your life means coming fully into your uniqueness as a human being. I am always in awe at the unending line of interesting and unique people I meet who have dreams and passions that are unlike anyone else I have ever met. It is only in taking full responsibility for all the choices in your life that you will allow yourself to unleash your full potential.

So, look around at your life and take full responsibility. See the physical things—like the beautiful home with the well-tended garden and the stuffed closets, laundry piled up. See the relationships—the beautifully rich ones with a few friends and the other ones lacking in care and authenticity. See the work that you do—the thoughtful, high quality work as well as the half-done and incomplete work. This is not about shame or feeling less than. In fact, taking responsibility for all of it can help us better understand why we have made the choices we have made in our physical space and in our relationships. But resist the urge, the overwhelming urge at times, to blame others. Stop blaming your parents, your spouse, your kids, your friends, your employer, your neighbors and take 100% responsibility for your choices. It may take a few tries to really allow yourself to feel the sense of responsibility for your own life, but it will be transformational. Because once we realize we are responsible, then we are completely empowered to make the changes we see fit to move in the direction of our dreams. The extent we allow ourselves to be held back by others is exactly the extent we will not make the changes that are calling to be made. This process of accepting responsibility, releasing all blame, can be done quickly or again; it can take a lifetime to fully embody it. The choice is up to you.

You Can Only Change You.

Early in my coaching career, I would spend many sessions with clients listening to them explain all the problems they saw with the company, their boss, their boss's boss, their peers, their team members, etc. It would take me a long time (and sometimes we would not get there) to get to the point of insight around their own role in the situations they were concerned about and their opportunities for leverage. Now, many years later, I am still interested in the context in which people are operating that includes their assessment of the motives and behaviors of those who work closely with them; however, I am able to help people much more quickly understand and accept that blame will not get them any closer to their goals and that their greatest leverage point is their own mindset and behaviors and they will never be able to change others directly. Thus, we can have much more productive conversations around how they are viewing the situations they find themselves in and what opportunities and potentials exist to do things differently.

Where are the areas that we are not showing up for in our own lives? Where are the areas where we have deferred responsibility to others? Where are the areas where we make excuses for our poor behavior because of circumstances or others? We tell ourselves that we would be different if they would be different. We would not talk behind other people's backs at work if others didn't already do it. We would not argue with our children or our spouses if they weren't so stubborn and disrespectful. To gain our true clarity and purpose, we must take back responsibility for all of it. Even if we have been given a tough hand and we have issues with how our parents raised us, or with the traumas we have faced, we must work through those issues, forgive where needed, and take our power back. As we take our power back, we must also take our responsibilities back.

Trash in the House

My 13-year-old chocolate Labrador is a great dog but occasionally still does things that drive us mad. An example of this happened the other day when we left the trash out in the kitchen, left the house, and he tore it all apart, leaving treats (like a taco with sauce) in special spots around the house. I came home to find the mess and after scolding the dog and picking up the mess, I immediately texted my husband to let him know that he had caused this problem since he had failed to take the garbage out the night before or in the morning—as I had asked him to do multiple times. He graciously said sorry and he thought it was funny about the taco. I fumed that he probably left it out on purpose so this would happen, and I would have to pick it up. As I reflect on this incident now as I write this chapter on Responsibility, what I immediately see is that I chose to make him responsible for taking out the trash as well as for what happened when he didn't. In fact, if I take 100% responsibility, the other way to look at this situation is that I am the one who filled up the last of that trash bag, tied it and put it in the kitchen. I could have walked the 50 steps to the garbage at any point the first day, that night or even the following morning, but I chose not to. I was the only one who left the dog alone for multiple hours with the bag in the kitchen, and therefore, the inevitable result of having to clean the mess was a logical likelihood given my failure to take responsibility. In trying to push my responsibility onto my husband, I let go of my own power to prevent the situation.

Once we take responsibility for ourselves, the next step is to see our roles in the lives that we encounter in our day to day. What you do to another, you do to yourself. What you damn, damns you back. What you judge, you become. When you live long enough and allow yourself to see it, these are truths that you will inevitably encounter. Ask yourself in what ways you are neglecting your 'brother', your neighbor, others and the answer will be all the same ways that you are neglecting yourself. For example, I realized that I was rarely present for others in the moment, that I was distracted and worried about what I needed to do, problems I needed to solve. This was probably (still may be) very frustrating for others, but when I look at this behavior deeply, I realize that I am not truly present for myself. My soul, my body, my self has needs and wants and is trying to get my attention and I am too busy trying to get to the next thing, complete my to do list, not disappoint anyone, that I rarely take the time to sit with myself and just listen. Life is a giant mirror. Our relationships and even all our daily interactions with others are set up by our souls to show us what needs attention and focus. Because of this, you absolutely do have a responsibility to the others you meet on your path. What your responsibility is to them is only known by you in your highest wisdom. So, no, there is no list of must dos here, but there is great opportunity for those that you meet to look deeply at what gifts of abundance you might have to share with them, and what gifts they might have to be shared with you. It is a grand adventure when you realize that each person, every single one, has come to receive a gift from you—could be just a smile or an encouraging word or a silent wish of good will and then to leave them alone to be in peace—and in return you will receive what they came to give you. It might be much more.

What happens when we ignore our relationships with others? We inadvertently turn away from ourselves. I know it sounds counter-intuitive, but it is not. If we can see the other as a direct reflection of oneself, it is a wonderful way to live. A revelation

I had recently is that God is in everything—not just in other human beings, but also in animals and birds—this I can grasp. But also, in the insects and plants—still getting this. But also, in the room, in the chairs, in the beds, in the walls—this gets harder to understand but it does not make it less so. God is the all of it, the up and down of it, the left and right of it, the high and low of it. The understanding of this changes everything. When you truly grasp this, you will feel at home in the world and at peace with your life.

You Are Your Neighbor's Keeper.

How many times do we watch a story of violent crime on TV where they interview the neighbors and the neighbors share a reaction of complete shock—"They always seemed so normal"—to knowing reflection—"It was just a matter of time"? While each person charts their own course in this life, the way many of us live and the way we raise our children is to think about themselves and to care for themselves and yet, if we see people in need in our homes, our neighborhoods, towns, states, countries, and even world, it is our responsibility to do something. That 'something' might be as simple as offering them a silent blessing and wishing them well, or it might be a grand action of engaging in others' lives directly. But regardless, I believe that we are united as a human system and while we are not responsible for 'fixing' others or for 'fixing' the world's problems, we are absolutely not expected to bury our heads in the sand and pretend that all we need to consider is ourselves.

So, love the one you are with! And feel that love returned. What about the bad ones? What about the ones that have hurt me or my family? What of those that are living wrong? What of them? Ask yourself these questions and you know the answer. The answer is you must love them too. God is in them too. They hurt as you hurt and in some very specific ways, they are a mirror of you, even if you would rather not see this. As I write this there was yet another mass shooting in the US. This time, I have a connection—not a close one—to the victims and the shooter. I am being tested to live what I believe: love them and pray for them. This is not easy, but it is simple, and it is time that we learn this lesson. As I turn away from anyone, I turn away from myself. You don't have to like what they have done, but in order to live your deepest truth, you must forgive and love the person. Because the love you give another, is the love that is given you.

We tend to focus on 'my' family, 'my' friends, 'my' religion, 'my' country and in order to take a step forward, we need to try to enlarge our circle to include everyone—all—regardless of their relationship to us. This is the healing the world needs and it is the same message that has been shared with us in all major religions, movies, books: We are all one and we must accept that no one, no matter the circumstance, is above or below any other. Consider this lesson of unity deeply and decide for yourself what is true.

All the madness we see in the world is but a reflection of areas that have been neglected by society. The movement (if you want to call it that) to finally pay attention to and stop stigmatizing mental health issues is long overdue. Partly this is because we did not see this as our responsibility. Many of us who have had our own mental health struggles or who have seen others challenged in this way know in a deep way the lack of support and resources that exist for most people. But this is not just the responsibility of those affected. This is our collective responsibility as a society. So, what does that mean for people like me and you? It means that we can't ignore issues we see around us that don't, yet, affect us directly. It means that we can make positive choices each day that will affect our own lives but also the lives of others. I am not talking about politics here, although that is an area where we can affect change by electing people into office who have a sense of responsibility to all people in our society, but it also means on a day to day basis, staying aware and open to those around us and how we might support them. I volunteer at a hospital with my dog who is a certified pet therapy dog and we often visit the behavioral health unit, otherwise known as the psych ward. One of my observations each time we visit is that those who are going through an acute mental health crisis often look and sound just like you and me. Some don't—some are more like what you have seen in movies—and yet most, other than the faraway stares or sadness in their eyes, look just the same as us. Most people, unfortunately, have had their own experience of themselves or of a loved one suffering with anxiety, depression or even suicide attempts. They also know that it is hard to know what is going on below the surface by looking at someone, and that these challenges transcend gender, age, race, ethnicity, and socioeconomic status.

Responsibility sounds like a heavy word and conjures up feelings of obligation and overwhelm. Some say to me, "If I can barely take care of myself and my family, how am I to be responsible for others?" And herein lies the beauty of the human experience. As we start to take the attention off ourselves and our small worlds and expand it to include others, the sense of connectedness to all things increases, which immediately decreases our feelings of both obligation and overwhelm. You don't have to believe me, yet I encourage you to try it out. For a day, a week if you can muster it, walk around and think to yourself, "What if I am responsible for that? For the neighborhood roads? For the homeless man on the corner? For the ocean in front of me?" What ideas does it bring up for you?

Diffusion of responsibility, also known as the bystander effect, is a concept in social psychology that demonstrates that people will act less responsibly when they believe there are many others who can 'do something' or become responsible rather than just them. If the same event occurred and the person was the only one there, they would surely do something because there is a clear need and no one around to help. Yet when there are many people witnessing an event, what happens is no one ends up helping as the responsibility is so diffused and often unspeakable atrocities go unconfronted due to a human tendency to expect someone else to take care of it. Thus, sometimes we do not feel responsible because we assume others have taken care of it—often others that are smarter than us, know more about the situation than us, have more means than us, or are more directly affected than us. It is interesting to note that those who are often the most generous are those who have been down on their luck in the past. It seems that we build empathy by experiencing the difficulties of others firsthand. When we have not had a particular experience—of being poor, being ill, being ostracized, losing our homes, losing our livelihoods, or being forced to leave our countries—it can be a stretch for us to really understand how difficult these situations can be. So, what is the remedy? The remedy is to understand that you are responsible; if you can see it, you have some responsibility to it. Now this is not meant to overwhelm you because I know when I look around at the sheer number of issues that are happening that I would have to take responsibility for, it make me want to go back to bed and get under the covers. And yet, I challenge you to think like this for a day or a week.

We are so focused on action in our society. What do we need to do? How do we need to fix it? There are many other ways to influence a situation positively that don't involve observable action. You can change your mindset and change the way you are seeing the situation. You can pray for solutions and for guidance for all. You can write about the situation to help others to gain new insights about it. You could have a conversation with others to ask questions to try to understand how they are seeing the situation. And yes, you can roll up your sleeves and take direct action to improve the situation. All of these can be fruitful, but often the most fruitful is to ask ourselves: If we are responsible for this in some way (and I contend we are if we can see it), what is within our power to help influence in a positive direction?

When there comes a time that others are in need and we are suitably in tune with ourselves, then we will be able to help. When this time comes, it will be said that we have finally moved forward as a society. Some have said that the measure of a society is what is done to the least of us is done to all of us. And in our society, many of us have wrongly concluded that it is every man for himself. It is not and it will never be. Again, do not be daunted by this. You can take baby steps in this direction in your own life. Walk through the day a little more aware: What does this moment need from you? Who is in the frame? What do they need that you may be able to gift them—a smile, a conversation, a hand to hold a bag that is too heavy for them, a seat that you don't need anyway? Look for these opportunities to be responsible for more than just yourself and your family and you will find that they are all around you. You will also find that the blessing you will receive by giving this gift is far more than what you would have expected.

Many people I talk to believe this to be extremely hard for them. It is only hard because we have been raised to 'mind our own business' and to worry about ourselves. But the truth is that while we should not worry about ourselves or others—worry does not get us anywhere productive—we must take responsibility for this life and not as narrowly as we have defined. Now this cannot be an excuse to get into others' business to tell them how to run their lives; it is still a situation where everyone has free will and your offer of assistance, help, prayers, should be neutral and help others to help themselves.

A Helping Hand.

I was at the airport, having arrived in Boston with two small children in tow—age 2 and 3—and a whole lot of luggage. As I tried to load the luggage onto a cart and called my husband on the phone to ask him to come pick us up, I had 2 overtired children attempting to run in different directions. I had asked them to stay close to me and grabbed them repeatedly when my 2-year-old, who thought this was a fun game, went running right out the doors 10 feet away from us that led outside to the road where hundreds of cars were buzzing by. Before I could stop him and as I stared in disbelief, a woman ran through the doors after him, scooped him up laughing and returned him to me. I thanked her quickly and then she was gone. I immediately felt like crying in gratitude, but it was only after she walked back to her own family and luggage that I realized that she was travelling alone with 4 children, all under the age of 6! At the time, I could not believe how kind it was for her to do that and I have thought about it many times since then, usually when I am travelling and see a mother or father struggling with young kids! There were dozens of people within the distance of my son at that moment, but it took this young mother, one presumably with empathy for my situation (and seemingly much better organization skills and better behaved children than me) to go out of her way for us. I am happy to report that I have experienced many versions of this type of kindness since then with people, often mothers, willing to help my kids and/or me at a moment's notice. The point is that it can be quite simple to do something that is meaningful for another person who is struggling, it is just that we are often so caught up in our own situation that we choose not to do this. We can always make a different choice.

What does it mean to develop character? Character development is all about taking responsibility for one's life and one's actions as well as the consequences of those actions. A person of high character is someone who can be trusted to be relied upon, to tell the truth, to show up, to confront even difficult things if it is the right thing to do. Character development is not language we use very often nowadays, but the concepts have never gone out of style. By taking more responsibility for ourselves and the society we find ourselves in, we will be setting a strong example of character development for our children to follow.

Let's make this practical for your life. What do you have to share? If you are an eternal being here to learn lessons and to share love, then what are the gifts you came to share? Material gifts, perhaps? For example, I have a lemon tree and a grapefruit tree in my front yard, and I have so many lemons and grapefruit that it is almost comical. But it was only when I started putting them in bags and having my daughter deliver them to neighbors that I realized the true blessing of the trees. I love lemons but only need a few a week and I don't even like grapefruit yet the tree has become a great blessing as we are excited to share the fruit with those who do love grapefruit and I am able to free my yard of all the fallen grapefruit that drop to the ground when they aren't picked. So, what can you give? Do you have a plethora of blankets you have been given as gifts that sit in a closet and never get used? Could you share them with the local homeless shelter? Or the SPCA where they are always looking for blankets? A one-time used 'special' dress like a baptism, wedding, or even prom dress that you loved but no longer have use for? Do you have extra books that your children have grown out of that you could share with a local school since they are always looking for books? Do you have a basketball hoop in your driveway that rarely gets used? Can you move it to the street where all the neighborhood kids can enjoy it whenever they want? We did this and it is so fun to watch how much more useful and valuable the hoop is now that there are three families that use it regularly. These may sound like small and simple ideas, and many of us have good intentions but we don't take the step to assess what we have an abundance of and how we might be able to share it.

Beyond material gifts, ultimately, we are asked to identify what specific gifts we have been given that we can share with others. Do we have relaxed dispositions that put others at ease and thus a simple walk down the road with smiles on our faces can lighten another's day? Are we exceptionally organized and could assist others, even informally, in getting themselves organized in order to achieve their goals? Are we great with communicating to children and could we spend one hour a week or one hour a month mentoring children at the local library? Do you have experience dealing effectively with an illness or challenge that you could share with others? What are your gifts and how can you use them? This attitude will help us go beyond the material reality that we tend to live in with the pressing issues of the day and help us create broader mindsets of abundance and gifts that the world is so sorely in need of. Where we can get stuck is thinking these have to be big things. They do not. They are small and yet they could be amazing gifts for someone who needs them. The answers will become apparent if we focus on the question: "What do I have to give today?" or "What do I have to give in this interaction?" Try it and see.

And what if I just want to sit at home and rest after taking care of my family? Then, that is fine and that is your choice. Still, I would ask you: What are your gifts and how might you share them at home with your family and your friends? Ultimately, we must start where we are and while I would encourage you to try to draw the circle wider than your immediate family, immediate neighborhood, or country of origin, it really does not matter where you start. Once you start believing you are more than the body that has been given to you (as a gift!), you will be led to better understand your gifts and your abundance, and you will be led, step by step to the sharing of those gifts to the perfect places and people. Such is the beauty of our lives: It only takes the intent, the willingness, the openness to see things differently for the path to appear.

You will know you are taking more responsibility in your life when you no longer find yourself blaming others for what happens or for difficult circumstances. You will see your role in your life more clearly and because of this, you will be more motivated to make small and sometimes big changes in how you approach each day, year, and decade. You will start doing things you always wanted to do instead of waiting for permission or for some theoretical future time because you realize you are the only architect of your life. You will give more of your time and attention to others in whatever ways feel right for you because you recognize that you are part of an interdependent system of people and you will be amazed at the opportunities that arise for supporting others. There will still be good and bad days, but you will be empowered to live the life you always intended.

QUESTIONS TO CONSIDER:

- If you were fully responsible for your life and there were no limitations, what would be different? What implications does this have for how you would live?
- What is one area of your life that you would like to take more responsibility for? Imagine that you are 100 % responsible. What implications does it have for how you think about the situation and/or the actions you might take?
- Where do you see yourself and/or your family as better or smarter than others? Where do you see yourself or your family as less than others? These are both forms of judgement that are not true and not helpful to your success. What would need to happen for you to truly see all people—regardless of any perceived difference—to be equal in all ways?
- Where are the areas of abundance in your life? How can you share this abundance with others?
- What are the gifts and talents you have been given? How do you share these gifts and talents in your daily life now? What could this look like in the future?

STEP 4
COURAGE

"The spiritual journey is the unlearning of fear and the acceptance of love."

Marianne Williamson

"Be not afraid."

John Michael Talbot

Fear leads our lives. We may not know it and if we do know it, we may not want to admit it. But it is everywhere, in our thoughts, in our words, in our external environments. To achieve clarity in your life, you must face the fears that you have allowed to dictate your life. This sounds scary, I know. But it need not be. Ask yourself, "What am I afraid of?" And then write a long list. Don't stop writing until you run out of things to say. Don't censor yourself and don't worry about the level of the answer: I'm afraid to call the hairdresser; I'm afraid he is going to leave me; I'm afraid they will be hurt or worse, die; I'm afraid that they will realize I am incompetent and don't know what I am doing; I am afraid my salad won't be good enough for the dinner. It doesn't matter what comes up; they are all equally useful in their own way. Now, don't let this exercise discourage you because like the chapter on honesty, once you realize all the fears that are just below the surface, it can feel like too much. But it is isn't. Allow each of the fears to be re-known by you in a higher way. How to do this? Ask the fear what purpose it is serving for you. It is there for a reason. Then thank it for coming and then allow it to be re-seen in a non-fearful way or released.

A life without fear is rare, but in such a life, fear is replaced by love and tolerance. We are afraid of the unknown and we are afraid of that which we don't understand. We have been raised like this for many, many generations and again, the fear may not release all at once. But if you allow yourself to, it will be removed for you. The purpose it has been serving is no longer useful and can be replaced by opportunity, opportunity to just be with what is. You need not be afraid of it. The truth is that you can't control it, so ask yourself what your role is in the thing you fear and you will be shown a way through it. "But what if I stop worrying, then won't all these things I worry about come to pass?" No, they won't. And in fact, they may be less likely to come to pass if you pass the concern for them over to God. Try it on one topic—for example, worrying about your kid's performance in school—just let it go. Letting it go it doesn't mean that you aren't still helping them with their homework; it means that when fearful thoughts enter, you notice them, offer them to God or the Universe or your Highest Self, and then let them go. The more you try this with the smaller things, the more your faith will grow that you never really had to worry anyway, and the more you will be able to do this with the big stuff too. Then you will really start to see changes in your life as you focus more on the things you are grateful for, you ask more questions about what is possible, and you enjoy each moment more.

What you fear, you attract. What you judge, judges you back. The important thing to understand here is that you need not be afraid of your thoughts or your fears. Thinking about this can make one paranoid about having negative or fearful thoughts and make things worse, not better! But the understanding of it is critical. Commonly in psychology, this is referred to as a self-fulfilling prophecy. Allow this truth to be revealed to you. Then show up and look your fears in the eye, which will reduce their power over you. You are the one in charge, and you do not need to live a life trapped in fear. I used to tell my kids that everyone has fears, every day. Bravery and courage are not living without fear, bravery and courage are feeling the fear and then doing it anyway. One fear at a time, do it anyway.

Courage is your birthright. Take one step forward in the direction of your dreams and then watch what happens. You must declare your intention and take a visible step forward and then not be deterred. This does not mean giving up your critical thinking and judgement in any situation, but it does mean challenging yourself to lean into the unknown far more than you have allowed yourself in the past. In my coaching work I see this all the time. We start working on something, the person makes a breakthrough in their mindset and starts to make small changes and then something significant changes in their world, in their context, which allows for this transformation to occur and for the potential to become a reality. It is hard to explain but it does happen. I don't pretend to fully understand it, but I am continuously amazed at how the Universe supports our efforts especially if we are truly committed to change. Thus, growth is all about stepping into the unknown and for most of us, the unknown is scary. As we set out into the unknown, we must let go of what we have known and letting go is not always our strong suit. We may encounter people and experiences along the way that we never thought we wanted—this is to be expected. It takes a certain amount of courage to keep stepping forward, but once you take a leap of faith and see all the beauty and benefits that come with that, it gets easier and easier to be courageous. If you stop before the beauty comes, it is like you have been invited to a wonderful party up on a hill overlooking the ocean. At this party, are beautiful people, music, food, all your favorite things. But you get lost on the way up the hill and just as you see the lights and start to pull into the driveway, you panic and think that the trip was too long, too painful, and what happens if you hate the party and the people, music, and food are different than you expected? So you turn around and go back down the hill. The moment of courage is to walk down the driveway, ideally smiling and in positive expectation, knock on the door, go in and enjoy the party! That is the moment of choice.

Sounds easy but for most people it is not. One reason is because we as humans have a long memory for tough times and tough situations from our pasts, maybe not consciously but in our bones, and these memories send out warning signals—be wary, be careful, things are not as they seem. It is a great protective mechanism, but it has outlived its usefulness. So, thank the system, thank it for the warning, and step forward in faith.

In my experience, courage often does not come in high profile actions where someone rushes into a burning building to save a baby. Mostly, courage happens over time, when we continuously choose to face what is easier not to face. To show up for those days and those experiences that we know may be difficult yet are important for our growth. To do the right thing, not the easy thing. Courage is almost never the path of least resistance and yet, what I have seen is that as people make these choices repeatedly, life and doing what needs to be done gets much easier. It is no longer as hard as it once was to have the difficult conversation, to say the thing that needs to be said, to stand up and put oneself out on a limb in front of a few or even many people. This is the gift of courage: Once the muscle is flexed repeatedly, it becomes strong and the energy that was once needed to engage at this level is no longer required. Thus, don't be overwhelmed by large acts of courage, but lean into what is hard for you today and know, *know*, that it will not be this hard forever. Even if no one else knows that you are being courageous by getting out of bed today or by showing up to work or by taking your child on a new playdate, you will know and these small acts are seen and registered as you build confidence and courage day to day. On the days or in the areas that are just too hard today, don't beat yourself up, let them go, and try again tomorrow.

Another relevant concept in psychology is that of 'self-handicapping,' which is defined as "a cognitive strategy by which people avoid effort in the hopes of keeping potential failure from hurting self-esteem." I have had my own experiences with self-handicapping. I was in training to become a yoga teacher and as such, it was recommended that I support my own yoga and meditation practice daily or at least most days of the week. I have had weeks where I don't practice at all due to a myriad of excuses—injury, too busy, don't have enough energy—and then the doubts come in: Can I really do this? How can I teach others when I am not even actively practicing myself? How can I teach others when some days I feel like I don't even have the energy to get through the day? It has been said that we 'teach that which we still need to learn' and for me, this is an important concept that helps me move past my fears of imperfection. I then thought to myself, OK, I may never be the yoga teacher I envisioned and my discipline can use some work; the fear has come true, now what? Who am in the face of this? Who do I choose to become? I choose to be fully present when I do practice and to enjoy the benefits for my sake and the sake of others. Doubts and victim consciousness be gone! Who will you become when you face your fears?

It takes courage to be in this world. This is a place of constant change, constant challenge, and for whatever reasons, we have not figured out how to live together peacefully, making it harder than it needs to be on ourselves and on our children. For this reason, for many people, just getting up in the morning can feel like an act of courage and it is. Each person's path is different and the way they handle those challenges is unique and yet there is a general lack of empathy and understanding in how tough it is for many others to just get through the day. You know the trials you face, and you know what it feels like when things are darkest for you. On these days, courage may simply look like getting up, getting showered, and showing up at work. Or it may look like making a phone call to your insurance provider to find the name of a psychologist or counselor that you can speak to about the challenges you are facing. Sometimes courage is just taking care of ourselves a little bit better than yesterday—one more glass of water, one more piece of fruit, a walk around the block, one less glass of wine. Whatever it is, it takes courage and you should recognize and acknowledge yourself for these small but important steps. In addition, courage can look like texting or calling a friend you know is having a hard time. It can be bringing up a conversation with your spouse, child, or coworker that you know may be a tough conversation but needs to happen. It can be calling a family member that you haven't spoken to in years to open the lines of communication again. It can mean sending an application in for a new job that you would like but aren't sure you are totally qualified for. It can mean talking to your new neighbor that you have never managed to have a conversation with before. There is no limit to the number of actions that take courage and some of these may seem small or big to you, but it does not matter. The courage is in doing what you want to do, believe you should do, need to do even if you are scared, tired, discouraged. The mistake we make is that somehow, we want to wait for the inspiration to hit us first and that is backwards. Take the step and the inspiration will come. Even if it doesn't, at least you took the step! But I suspect it will come for you. Then, as you get used to taking new and different steps that are out of your comfort zone, your comfort zone will expand which is exciting and it means your life will expand! But don't rest there. There are still more courageous steps for you to take. Ask what the next best steps for you are and then take those too!

You Attract What You Fear.

In psychology this is a well-known concept called 'self-fulfilling prophecy' and yet I have found many people that don't have any insight into the way their fears draw to them the very things they fear. I think of a mother I know who was so afraid that she would 'lose' her adult son to his new wife that she clung strongly to control of him, only to have the son push further and further away, realizing the situation she feared had come to pass. I think of a man in a relationship where his worst fear was for his girlfriend to cheat on him and thus, he also clung strongly to control—criticizing her when she went out with her friends, growing angry when she engaged in activities without him—only to find out that she wanted out of the relationship, so she could find someone who would be more accepting of her as she was. I think about the woman who was afraid she would never get promoted. She felt trapped and unappreciated and told many others that she would never get promoted in the current "unfair" system. When the time came for the team to discuss her promotion, all agreed she had the capabilities to do the job but her attitude and her maturity were not what was needed at the next level. Most of the fears we hold, especially the darkest ones where our children, our friends and our lives are suddenly cut short at the hand of a terrible accident or crime, thankfully, will never happen despite our worries. However, many of the smaller worries we hold, the ones that we cling to day in and day out, may be more likely to occur because of our unwillingness to look at our fears directly and to understand how our fears drive our behaviors and choices. Many people I work with want to be more 'free' and when we dig deep to understand what freedom means, it really means that they want to be free from fear. The good news is that we can release fear when we choose to.

What is happening now in our society is an escalation of fear-driven control and yet with this escalation, I feel hopeful that many people are able to see the pattern more clearly. There is always a choice to make and many movies and books and great leaders throughout time have told us the same thing: we must choose fear or love; we cannot choose both. When presented this choice, most people say that they would of course choose love and yet this is not always true for us as individuals and it is unfortunately not always true for us as a society either. Fear is powerful and I have never met anyone who has not been completely frozen in fear at one time or another in their lives. These fear memories live on and we must consciously decide it is OK to release them and let them be replaced by love. This is why all the major religions talk about forgiveness. Forgiveness is directly related to releasing the trapped energy of fear in oneself. After coaching many people over many years, I know that fear is insidious and often does not show its face directly, rather it comes up in us as judgement of others, playing small, being critical, and being prudent. When we act in these ways, it is socially acceptable, and we do not recognize that we are making choices out of fear. As with most things, it is easier for us to identify these actions as fear in others but for ourselves, we do not see it in this way. So, what can we do about this? We can continue to challenge our own thoughts and choices. What is driving this decision? Am I running away from something (read: fear)? Or am I running toward something (read: opportunity)? We can push ourselves to feel the fear and do it anyway and with each time we do this, we realize that the world did not end, and we are still here. Even if we take risks that don't work out, we can learn that it is OK for some things not to work out. It is important that we challenge ourselves in this way, otherwise we continue the cycle of fear with our own children.

People confuse courage with bravado all the time. The louder and more forceful someone appears, the more courageous we think they are, but this could not be further from the truth. True courage, real courage is not as easy to identify or as easy to see from the outside. Most of the time we have no idea of the inner or outer challenges and struggles each person has overcome and is currently facing. We have no awareness of the courage it takes for some to stand up for themselves or stand up for another. We have no awareness of the courage it takes to choose life over the debilitating effects of an illness or to choose life after an incredible loss. We are much more equipped to see the courage in ourselves: the times that we have risen to the occasion to finish a project, support a friend, stand up for someone when we didn't think we could, or it would have been easier to ignore the situation. Small moments of courage happen each day for all of us and the more we can recognize these, the more they can build momentum and before you know it, we are living a courageous life. Of course, what that means for each of us is different, and yet the commonality is to stay aware of the opportunities that present themselves and to choose the harder way, if it is right, than to always choose the path of least resistance. How do we teach courage to our children? As with most of the steps to clarity, our best tool, our best approach is to identify what courage is for ourselves and then to live it. We can also challenge our children, family, and our friends to reflect on who they choose to be and to allow their lives to reflect this choice.

When you hear the word 'should' let it be a wakeup call. Before you accept something from your perspective or others'—that something should be done in a particular way, said in a particular way, that you should wear this or that—take some time to question this assumption. Who says it should be done in that way? Why do they say that? Do you even agree with it? Why or why not? What if it was done in a different way? Could that be better? Or perhaps not better, but is it OK if it were different? Most of us drastically underestimate the degree to which societal, family, and friend 'shoulds' play into our day to day decision making. I 'should' bring all my clothes to the dry cleaners, I 'should' wash my car each weekend, I 'should' make sure that the kids are enrolled in enough extra-curricular activities. I am not suggesting any of these things are wrong, but rather that it is healthy and helpful for each of us to stop taking the 'shoulds' at face value, and instead to really challenge ourselves and when appropriate, others, to make decisions based on our own current realities instead of reacting from the fears or even opportunities of the past. Similar advice is to be given for all the 'should nots'. We 'should not' spend all our money before retirement. We 'should not' walk barefoot outside. We 'should not' let the kids decide. The list could go on and on, but again, the point is not the content of the list; it is the content of your list of shoulds and should nots that drives your behavior. Imagine that you are moving to a new country and you are encouraged to ask lots of questions about why things are done the way they are so that you can then decide, as a new citizen of another country, which behaviors are helpful for you and which are not. Yes, it does take courage to move against the shoulds of your family, of your culture, and of your habits. There is much energy in our typical habit patterns and so you must be strong and courage must be present to make the changes. However, once you really understand what you want to change and why, not only will it come easier for you, but the universe will seem to conspire to help you get exactly the life you are seeking.

How will you know when you are living your life without fear? Well, this one is easy. You will feel completely free. The freedom that many of us are striving for through other means—financial freedom, complete independence from others—if we go down a few layers, what we really aspire to is freedom from all fears. Small, steady steps in this direction look like: when you feel fear about something and you do it anyway. Regardless of the outcome, you lean into the fears. You do not allow your fears to dictate your day and you become less reactive in your interactions with others. You are not afraid of other people. This is an interesting one for the life and times we live in where the news, whether fake or not, is heavily focused on the negative, things that scare us, problems in our society and so it creates the impression that we live in a world full of dangers at every turn. I could lament here the differences between the way many of us were raised in the '70s and '80s compared to how we raise our children now (I currently have 2 elementary-age kids, so I live with this tension all the time). We, as a society, have moved in the direction of accepting fear as a way of life and try to exert control to keep the attackers at bay and yet we find ourselves with less and less real freedom. This way of life creates a culture of fear that is insidious and while we may not be able to control others, we can and should control our own lives by boldly and with faith making the choices we know to be right for us!

QUESTIONS TO CONSIDER:

- How do I define courage? What would it look like if I were leading a more courageous life?
- What am I afraid of? Make a list of all things large and small. Put the list down for 10 minutes, pick it up again, and keep writing. You may even be surprised by some of what shows up on the list. It is not necessary to understand why all these things are on the list, only to note that each and every one of them is putting a limit on your life while it remains.
- For each item on the list, ask yourself:
- What purpose does this fear serve for me?
- What is my role in creating this fear?
- Who am I without this fear?
- Am I willing to let it go?
- What are the 'shoulds' that are dictating my current life? Are there any that I am willing to release for myself? If so, what freedom will this allow?
- What one brave action can I take today to move in the direction of facing my fears, and as a result, live my most clear and purposeful life?

STEP 5
ACCEPTANCE

"Accept what is, let go of what was, and have faith in what will be."

Buddha

"The more you know who you are and what you want, the less you let things upset you."

Stephanie Perkins

If you were to plot out all that has happened in your life, how much of it did you plan? 50%? 80%? 20%? It doesn't matter. The point here is that some percentage of your life was not planned; it just happened. For most people the unplanned part is the higher percentage. "Well, I didn't see that coming!" Life is a mystery. "We plan and God laughs," goes the saying. Many of life's books, plays, and movies show us that we need to be open and accepting of the way life is, and not spend all our energy trying to control the day, the lessons we receive, and most importantly the other 'actors' in our lives' plays.

Lives are fluid and the tides come and go, just like in the sea and so while it is true that you create your life from your energy, your intentions, it is also true that you cannot easily predict the seasons or the happenings and this is where acceptance comes in. To have clarity in your life, you must accept that what is happening is happening, and yet not attach to it. It is happening and you must respond—or not respond—but keep an attitude of "this too shall pass" because the surest way to keep an issue or challenge stuck in place is to engage fully with it and fight against it. Fighting or resisting something will keep it firmly in place. But what about those things we feel we must fight—illness, injustice, lies? Accept these things as they are and then choose again, choose differently. It is a subtle but important difference. This is not a teaching of denial in any way; it is a teaching of honesty. Be honest with yourself about what is, look at it directly, and do not shy away. And then choose best how to deal with it, confidently and with purpose, and this is how you live your best life.

Accept what is. There is power in seeing what is in front of you and not resisting it. The next step beyond acceptance is enthusiasm, even gratitude, which is extremely powerful, and yet you would be amazed by the energy you would save and the power you would have if you simply stopped resisting what shows up in your life.

Acceptance is easy for the 'good things' most people tell me, but not easy for the 'bad things'. However, if you really think about your life, can you really tell, when something is happening, whether it is a 'good thing' or a 'bad thing'? Most people, myself included, can look back on times in their lives that were extremely difficult or painful and find the nuggets of beauty and learning that came of these and come to believe that it was a 'blessing in disguise' or at the very least, an important journey that one would not walk away from because of all that came after. If you really think about it, in our limited perspectives, we have no real anchor to determine whether anything that shows up in our day—a chance encounter, a new job offer, an email from a former acquaintance, a mistake on our phone bill, a C on our child's report card, a cancelled appointment, an illness—is really, ultimately 'good' or 'bad'. Therefore, my recommendation is to treat it all as though it is exactly as it should be. The argument against this, of course, is that if we fully accept what shows up, then we will become complacent, or worse, lazy and therefore we will not strive for better than what we have today. Yet, the irony is that what makes us complacent, what robs us of our power, is our inability to see, to truly acknowledge the current state of things. As is often said, the first step to solving a problem is admitting you have one. So, stop pushing, denying, resisting, fighting and see, allow, accept what is happening. Then, you are in the most powerful position to move forward.

Another key to the teaching of acceptance is that it works best if you can accept the small things and the big things. In some ways, it is easier to understand the teaching for the big things that we just spoke about—illness, death of a loved one, etc. Most people see fairly clearly they have no choice but to accept the situation. But day to day preferences for how the day should go, how people should treat you at the store, how your kids should behave in front of the neighbors, how the food should taste when you eat out, these are also opportunities for acceptance that we often resist or fight against because we want to hold our 'standards' for how things should be. I also struggle with this and yet I see it so clearly when working with others that these day to day decisions are where the rubber meets the road on whether we create a joyous or disappointing life for ourselves. So, what happens if you accept that the service at your favorite restaurant is quite poor today? Well, for one it does not mean that you cannot take any action—of course, you can still send your meal back or share your feedback with the manager. This is not a lesson in inaction. However, it does mean that after you take the appropriate action, you *let it go*. That's right, you let go of the situation and you don't stew about it all day, call all your friends, and post on social media about the situation at the restaurant. You accept what happened, you take appropriate action, and you let it go. Let's take a more challenging situation: an argument with your spouse. While you don't like his or her point of view, you must accept there is a disagreement, you choose what to do about it, and then you let go of outcomes. This is a critical lesson that may take a while to learn or you may already get it—in which case you know how beneficial it is to live this way.

It was always fairly easy for me to enjoy this level of acceptance in a work setting. Maybe because of my psychology training or my fairly diplomatic personality, but for years people would ask me why I never got ruffled at work and it was because it was easy for me to be just a little detached—enough to see what was going on, not take things personally, and respond without getting too emotionally hooked. This has not been the case for me with my family, however, and I have had to learn this lesson the hard way (still learning!) in those circumstances.

Overwhelm is a feeling one can get when we are not fully in acceptance of our lives. If this is a challenge for you, remember that there will always be more to do than can be done and you might as well accept this truth and come to peace with it. There is no finish line and things will never be totally completed and in their proper place. Ask any mother or father who is responsible for the laundry in a family of four or more. It is literally an impossible task to have a moment when all the laundry is done and folded. Just as it could happen, here comes another pair of dirty socks, underwear, workout clothes, etc. Same with dishes. Same with dust on the floor. Or cleaning up kids' toys. Same with email. Same with bills. Now this could sound depressing, but it isn't. Once we realize that all things are in motion, including us, we can relax and enjoy the motion more than when we thought we were supposed to get to the end of the day and get an A.

So, how to handle this common challenge? Get focused and clear on what you absolutely must do and what you love to do and then create a life that allows you the maximum degrees of freedom to spend time on these things. Accept that you are at cause in your life, so you are the one who gets to set the rules—all of them—about who you are, how you will live, and yes, how you will spend your time. So, cut out those things that are not adding value. For some of us, that might mean shutting off the TV or stepping away from the computer to go out for a walk. It might mean leaving work an hour early to go wander around a bookstore. It could even mean finding the place in the world you have always wanted to go, determining how much it will cost, saving the money, booking the tickets, and going! Many of us have so many things that we need to do (work, take care of kids, clean house, pay bills, exercise) and things we like to do (read, watch TV, write, listen to music, visit with friends, play with kids), and things we want to do (travel, gardening, hiking, volunteering) that we end up jamming too much into a single day or week and end up feeling exhausted and wishing we had more time. Or we are barely able to do all the things we must do, so we never get to the things that we like to do or want to do and so we feel tired and unfulfilled. Acknowledge and accept that there are only so many hours in a week and then be focused and present with each hour as it comes. Each day remind yourself that this is your life and you are empowered to determine what is most important. Once you have done that, you can more fully engage with and accept what shows up!

Tools for Greater Acceptance.

How to accept is one of the questions I receive most. Most people want to do this, and they want to let go but it doesn't feel easy. In fact, to many, it feels impossible. A few techniques that I have found most helpful for myself and for my clients are:

- Breathe, just breathe. Breathing is one of the most powerful mechanisms for our release from all anxiety and discomfort. And yet until recently we never even considered teaching our children how to breathe deeply or how to use the power of their breath to relax themselves. Try deep breathing regularly and you will not be disappointed.

- Say thank you to *all* of it! This way of living with constant gratitude is not obvious to us. We think that we need to resist what shows up if we don't like it, and in particular, if we want to change it. This is not true. We need to accept all of it—and then choose again. The way forward is through, not around. So, look and listen to all that shows up in your day—in your body, in your energy, in your environment, in your relationships, and welcome it all! If you find something, a relationship perhaps, that doesn't feel good for any reason, thank the relationship and thank the person as they have just given you a great gift! There is something to explore here, there is something to release here. You must learn to love all of it. This is not nearly as hard as it sounds. This is how you are born. But your judgement and your fear get in the way. These things have been constructed and conditioned over time and they dictate much of your reactions, thoughts, and interactions. To find your true self and live your best life, you must release them.

- Don't take it personally. Many things seem personal, they seem as if they are all about us. The way a spouse or child talks to us. The way our boss looks at us when we hand her a report that we think she disapproves of. The way a parent talks about how we should call more often. While these things feel personal to us, in fact they are not. Yes, these situations do involve us, but we need not take the other person's emotions on. We would be well-served to observe the behaviors, notice the facial expressions, the words. In addition, we should play detective with more subtle changes during these interactions, like how we are feeling inside our body, the thoughts that are running through our heads. We should do this and observe it the same way we watch a movie, with a slight distance that will allow us to stay objective, and to not take things so personally. Doing this regularly takes practice and it takes time, but it will go a long way to helping you to accept all aspects of your life, all aspects of your day.

- Help someone else find greater acceptance. It is true that you get what you give. If you are struggling to find acceptance in areas of your life, take the focus off yourself and try helping someone else who is in a similar situation. For example, if you have an injury or disability that you can't come to grips with, then find someone else in a similar situation and see how you can help them be more comfortable and confident in their situation. This practice will help you gain a wider perspective on the issue and ideally, it will help you find the acceptance you are looking for. Remember, we teach that which we still need to learn!

For a real world example, let's imagine you are walking down the street and the woman passing you by scowls at you or ignores you. You may feel a sense of discomfort, then you have thoughts of how rude she is, how rude people in this town are, and underneath it, if you stay really aware, there is a fear, an anxiousness, that you are not good enough. There is something about you that she is judging, or doesn't accept, or doesn't see and this disturbs you to the core. You go home and tell your spouse a story about the mean, judgmental woman and you try to make yourself feel better by putting yourself into a position of superiority over her. Sound familiar? It should; we all do it in many interactions and in many forms. Let's try it from a different angle. We see the woman, she scowls at us, so we try smiling. She's still scowling, and passes us without a word. The body starts to feel uncomfortable and the mind connects to 'how rude'. Now at this juncture, there is an opportunity. An opportunity to notice what is going on in your body - how you are having shortness of breath, how you are not actually as in touch with your body as you were a minute ago. You connect to the breath. You breathe deeply. You 'see' the thought about her being rude, but you do not attach to it. You let it come and then go. The next thought comes which is that she must be judging you in some way. You breathe deeply into this thought, and immediately know in your gut that this thought is false. You watch it float by. Then if you are patient, the deeper thoughts come, that you have seen this type of woman before, that you are not worthy of being seen by her or by anyone. You take a deep breath now and allow the breath to free the anxiety that has coursed through your entire being. This thought is also not true. You release it. New thoughts may come. She is probably just in a hurry. Maybe she is feeling sad or scared today. You breathe through these as they are also just thoughts. More empowering perhaps but still made up. You breathe again and this time say thank you—to God, to the Universe, to your Higher Self—for that exchange. You feel much better—in your body and in your thoughts now. Breathe again.

Try this for a few days and you will find that it can really help you enjoy your day more and stay present in the moment. Now what about the 'big things', the unwelcome things, the real disruptions to the day or week or year or life? How to accept these things? The answer is the same. You must accept them, you must be grateful for them, and you must not resist them. Again, this does not, contrary to popular opinion, secure them in place. What it does is put you in concert with the true self who knows what this lesson is about and knows how to best, most easily, and most productively maneuver through it. This is something you must learn by doing. You, like me, can read 1000 books on the topic (which I have) and yet, until you start practicing, practicing, practicing, you will not make great progress in achieving the freedom that is rightfully yours.

What you resist, persists. This is perhaps one of the most significant and useful teachings I have ever heard, and I have observed the truth of this in myself and many of my clients over the years. Learning how to fully accept challenging situations can entirely change the outcome. Have you ever really struggled with a person at work? You spend time trying to make things better, but you also spend a lot of time and mental energy unhappy with the situation, talking to yourself or others about the challenges you have with the person or situation. And then the situation lingers, and lingers. Ultimately, you may leave the situation, or the other person may leave, but there is opportunity here. There is the potential for learning and growth. There is also opportunity to not get stuck, to not more firmly entrench the problem, which is exactly what we do when we put negative attention or negative energy on something. Here is where there is confusion. Acceptance is not the same as continuously repeating your version of the story to yourself or others. Calling a friend and sharing your story and all the problems so that they can help you decide what to do, does not sound like it is negative. But it is not productive in the sense that repeating the situation and the story, with all the negative emotions being felt again, can negatively affect you and the situation. What are the alternatives? You must acknowledge and accept fully the situation and the body sensations and thoughts associated with it. You must breathe through these as we have said. Then pay attention, get very quiet, go for a walk if you don't like meditating, but be confident that you will learn what you need to learn of the situation and then it will release. Don't try to drive the situation to a particular closure or try too hard to control it (easier said than done, I know). And what of asking your friend for advice? I won't tell you not to do it, but your guidance on how to handle this situation, what to feel about it, what to say, or do is within you! Once you have accepted the situation, gotten quiet, and asked these questions of yourself, you may hear what others have to say. But do not give away your own power or authority to others who will never have the perspective on your life and your lessons that you do.

Through is the way. When you feel out of control or you feel a bubbling up of anger, these are emotions you need to accept fully. Most of the time we teach our children that they should not have negative emotions, that they should not only not have them, but they definitely should not express them. These well-intentioned lessons can have unintended consequences where people learn to 'stuff' their emotions, to push them down until there is a safe time to take them out, or worse, stuff them for good. These emotions don't leave us in this case, they just lie in wait for another opportunity to come out. This is why road rage is even a thing. The people who are so angry inside that all it takes is a surface-level altercation with another driver to bring out their homicidal tendencies are people who have not learned how to process healthy emotions. This is sadly almost a societal epidemic. Sometimes these emotions are turned inward on ourselves (depression, suicide) or onto others (blaming, violence) or we just do whatever we can to numb them (drinking, drugs, over-eating). The key is to become aware of what is inside of you and to let it go. Let it move through you. Yes, it can feel scary if you have never allowed this very natural process to happen by engaging in the damaging behaviors mentioned; however, it can absolutely be learned. Ultimately, it is about being present, feeling it, and allowing it to release, whatever it is. The fear that we don't want to see the emotions, don't want to feel the pain, would not know what to do with it when it surfaces, is a lot of why we continue to push these things down or away. Yet, they will continue to come up because your healing is in the release.

You are not all those stuffed emotions and you need not feel shame for having them. As I just said, this is almost an epidemic in our country and in our world. See the emotions, accept them, and release them.

Accepting a Chronic Illness.

Acceptance can be extremely hard when it comes to our loved ones, especially our children. We were on a family road trip right after the kids got out of school for summer. My 10-year-old got very sick—up all night throwing up and zero energy. A trip to the out of town ER resulted in a medical transport to a pediatric intensive care unit and a Type 1 diabetes diagnosis. Even though doctors were very clear about the diagnosis as an autoimmune disease, the implications for insulin management and her future, it took weeks before I fully accepted the situation. Despite our best efforts to see, allow, and accept, it is not always simple as there are many defense mechanisms at play (e.g., denial, compartmentalization, rationalization). The way we have found through this trial is not to accept a lesser future for her as she learns how to handle this chronic illness, but rather to accept fully the challenge that has been placed in front of her and even find opportunities for gratitude. The courage she has shown along with the concern and offers of support from strangers who reached out to share similar stories were amazing gifts during the months that followed her diagnosis when things seemed most confusing. Even now, I am thankful for the opportunity for her and our family to grow from the challenge in new and different ways. Already I feel that she and we are being called to be more present and responsible for the body's needs as well as more empathetic to the health challenges that others face, both things that we took for granted before this experience.

What of the things of ourselves that we don't like, or we really hate? The secret habits we have that no one knows, that we are embarrassed about, or worse that we feel are shameful or make us less than we would otherwise be? We must practice complete acceptance of these as well. This is such a powerful teaching if we let it be. Those things that we hate about ourselves are the very same things that we see, judge, and hate in others. When we get an emotional charge or view something someone says or does in a judgmental way, it is almost always because they are reminding us in some unconscious way of something that we don't accept about ourselves or something we have not yet processed for ourselves. When we react with strong negative emotion to a person, a place, or an event, then the best way to handle it is to breathe deeply, breathe through it, accept it, and let it teach you what it means for you. In this way, you go into curiosity and put yourself into the role of learner.

You will know you have mastered acceptance when you are not ruffled by the day to day changes and situations that arise. You will not turn into a robot without emotion, but rather as things happen that at one time you might have called 'bad' or 'disappointing', you will now accept as what they are—the challenges of this day. They are the 'stuff' of your life, the clay that you get to mold into whatever you wish. You will even be grateful for all or most of it, even if you would have 'chosen' something different. You will know you are in acceptance when you look at yourself, your family, your friends without judgement and learn to meet them where they are. You will know you are in acceptance when you no longer spend time or energy discussing what went wrong and how you wish it could be different. You will be wide-eyed and clear in your approach to each day and understand that you are not the things that happen to you or around you but that you have complete free will to choose how you respond to them. As with the other steps, this is a journey and not a destination, but inevitably you will remain calm when the unexpected happens, be more resilient, and be more open to the changes that come. Finally, you will know you are in acceptance when more than anything else you feel peace in your heart, in your body, even during what you would describe as the toughest times.

QUESTIONS TO CONSIDER:

- What parts of your life are you in acceptance of? Where are you not at ease? Make a list of 10–15 things you wish were different than they are. Now let those wishes go. Breathe through the desire and the longing and whatever other emotions come up. This is what some have described as radical acceptance and some people find it very hard. In reality, it is not hard, it is simple, yet the acceptance must be found in the moment. What would one day of radical acceptance look like for you? Are you willing to try it for one day?

- As you go about your day, note the things that you find unwelcome or distasteful; are you able to accept them anyway? Could you even practice gratitude for the things that don't turn out the way you would want them? This is the fastest route to changing your experience, although many have learned the habit of pushing against that which shows up, not realizing this practice is the surefire way to hold it firmly in place.

- When someone you know, a friend or colleague, or even someone in a news story, does or says something that you don't approve of, that you 'would never ever do', feel what is going on in your body. Ask the question: "What is here for me to learn from?" Know that this judgement you are feeling can be a gift, a true gift, to you to see where there are blockages or challenges that you still need to release. Let them go; they are no longer serving you.

- Make a list of your judgements of others—specific others, like family members or coworkers, and more general others as well (e.g., people who are lazy, people who cut you off in traffic, criminals, those in that political party that you disagree with). Push yourself to be honest and write it all down. What does it mean to release these judgements? Now, review the list and say a quiet wish of good fortune and many blessings to each individual and group. How does that feel? Is there resistance inside of you? If so, where? If willing, continue to send blessings to these individuals and groups every day for 10 days; see if anything changes. Does the resistance lessen?
- What do you judge about yourself? Make a list and let the list be created and don't judge the list! Consider how judging yourself in these ways has served you. How has it not served you? What would it feel like to release these judgements?

STEP 6
SURRENDER

"Peace requires us to surrender our illusions of control."

Jack Kornfield

"My Soul is My Guide."

Rumi

Surrender is a process of allowing yourself to be guided to a higher place, a different place, than where you live most of the time. It does mean releasing control, but there is nothing scary about it since you are releasing control to a higher part of yourself, a wider part, and a part of you that knows more than you do and can look around corners a lot better than you can.

Surrender is all about letting go. Letting go of the specific expectations you have for this life. Letting go—not of your dreams—but of the way that those dreams must show up. Letting go of the past, which includes the pain, hurt, anger, sadness that you have been holding onto for so long. Letting go of the need to control every detail of your life, and harder, of the lives of others. Letting go of the judgements, the superiority, the inferiority, the not knowing.

Surrender is about letting go of all of these things so that they can be replaced by a quiet, confident knowing and peace that each step, each day, each hour is a valuable part of your journey. In time, letting go is replaced by faith that you are exactly where you are supposed to be. I like to think of it as surrendering to the 'truth of you'. We can surrender our entire lives or more often, we choose to surrender parts of ourselves or parts of our lives when we feel ready to do so. "Dear God or Dear Higher Self, please take the burden of this illness off of me. I can no longer bear it." As we surrender and let go of each burden, it will be lifted and we will feel a lightening, a sense of freedom. This type of surrender will take courage and yet, it can be extremely transformational for your life.

Like with the other steps, surrender can happen in an instant but for most of us, it will happen in stages as we acknowledge and allow the releasing. While this step is related to the others, especially acceptance, it may not feel as straightforward. There are some practical concepts that can help us prepare to surrender in order to find the clarity that comes with allowing our highest, best selves to take the wheel. These concepts include: living fully in the moment, finding your flow, and giving and receiving love.

One key to surrender is to live more in the present moment because it is in the present moment that your power lies. Try connecting to your Highest Self in this moment and see what happens. Even a small taste of being fully present in a work team meeting or a conversation with a friend can help you realize the extent to which you are multi-tasking through your life and short-cutting the richness of it. Try slowing down, try not *doing* so much and check in on what you are *being*. Try breathing more deeply. Try listening with your whole body—not just your ears but your heart and soul as well. Pay attention, notice what is happening, and if you can, be grateful for this moment—whatever is happening!

Life is lived in the past and in the future for many of us. Rarely do we fully tap into the potential of the present moment—mind, body, and spirit and because of this, we miss a lot. We bring so much of our previous experiences and judgements with us that we miss many opportunities and many moments where we could see beauty and opportunity with fresh eyes. Why is this? We are scared to be fully present. We have learned that it is safer to stay in the past, to be in our heads, to put one foot in, not to care too much, lest we get hurt. These painful emotions are what we are trying to avoid. However, as we avoid the painful emotions, we also avoid the joy and the grace. We can't have one fully without the other.

Being in the present moment can be uncomfortable. "My stomach hurts, my mind keeps wandering to my to-do list..." These are discomforts that we want to avoid so we put our minds on something else and 'suck up the pain', when in fact those discomforts are waiting for your attention. In my case, for many years, when I became fully present in the moment, I felt a welling up of emotions and often a need to cry. Sometimes gratitude wells up but more often than not, sadness. I don't know where the sadness came from, but it was there. I first consciously noticed it lurking below the surface when I had my first child and was home with a newborn. What is that level of sadness and anxiety that I feel all the time? I don't remember feeling this before. I think it was always there, or at least there from a young age, but I had spent years being so busy that I didn't need to attend to it. I started working when I was 15 years old and I had never taken significant time off since. Literally when I changed jobs, I did so by stopping work on a Friday and starting the new job on a Monday. I finally realized I was scared to be alone with myself in the present moment. This revelation was amazing to me given that if you asked me to write a list of things I enjoy most, being by myself might be top of the list. However, I had built a life that had made that next to impossible until the last few years.

Since it can be so uncomfortable, what are the benefits? There are many books and even religions that touch on this topic more deeply but simply, the benefit is that the present moment is where your life is. And the 7 steps to clarity outlined in this book can only be practiced in the present moment. (For example, put 'Ask questions about my day' on the to-do list for a week from Monday and see how well that works.)

There are times in your life when things come easy, smooth, without much effort. Some people call this grace and it is. But it is also what we know in psychology as flow, getting into the stream of what is meant to be, the river of life as they say. Flow is a concept that has been around for decades and yet we still don't teach this to our children in schools. There is a way of tapping into our higher potentials—in each moment—that is as straightforward as hooking up to a new energy source. When we know how to surrender to our Higher Selves, we can do things that almost seem miraculous—we can work faster and with more accuracy, we can solve difficult problems quickly, some of us can write beautiful music, or create inspiring art, or play sports at an inspiring level. If this is true, why don't we do it? Again, there is no need to blame but as a society we have not valued this aspect of ourselves and we have so many things that we need to do, and so many distractions, that only some people—at some points in their lives—really invest in this state of being.

You can see flow naturally in children. When they get so engaged in something, they will joyfully do it for hours. I had this experience a few times when I was in graduate school—in particular when I had to finally sit down and write my dissertation, I was 'taken away' by how easy and free flowing it was, after the dozens of times I sat down and resisted. I also had it happen a few times while running. Even the writing of this book has been a great flow for me. But this is not a concept that is true for a few people or even most people, it is available to *all* people and amazingly, it is available *all* the time.

How does one get into flow? It does have to do with being fully present in the current moment and allowing yourself to let go and surrender body, mind, and soul to whatever it is you are doing. My experience is that some people have done this all their lives and therefore it happens quickly and easily and, in many areas, many of us have had to learn to focus in this deeper way and allow the flow to come. Flow can also teach us what we are passionate about. For many of us, we had glimpses of this when we were young, those areas that came naturally to us and we loved. For me, this was writing. I used to write stories and plays and even won a few writing contests that still make me proud to recollect. For others it was painting or singing or playing music. Now, often our lives go in different directions and get more complicated and we forget the simple joy we had doing these things until much later when we realize that it is completely within our power to play again, to sing, to dance, to write or to do whatever it is that we love to do.

Another truth is that we can find flow in anything we do— anything! I am still working on this one as while I know it to be true, I still find myself struggling to find flow in the laundry and the dishes daily. But I have had glimpses of it, and I know people—certainly monks would be among this group but I know real, 'normal' people as well—who are able to allow this flow into their day to day activities.

Again, one of the messages of this book is that you are unique and that's why I say you need to surrender to the 'truth of you'. I do not believe that there is one way to eat, one way to pray, one way to raise your kids, one way to live or love. I believe that we are called to find the Way for ourselves, and one of the markers that we are going in the right direction is the feeling of flow. And it is a joy.

Where will you not find flow and thus not find yourself? You will not find it on your phone, on Facebook or Instagram. You may find it in your work, but the key is to know the difference between working for passion which can cause flow and working for addiction or from fear of failure. This gets back to the question of why; ask yourself, "Why am I working 10 hours a day on this book? Is it because it is an act of love or is it because I am afraid if I don't, I will never be anyone of consequence in this world?" At first, the answers may not be clear. But keep asking them and you will come to know what is true for you. With this information, you can make changes. Either change what you are working on or change why you are working on it.

There are days where things seem easier, where flow comes more easily and then there are the other days, the darker days for whatever reason. The extent to which you can continue to be present and allow what is going on inside of you and outside of you to occur, determines how fast you will grow and how soon you will be lifted beyond the struggle of that particular day or issue. The pain that you feel coming up on these days wants to be seen, it wants to be known, and it really wants to be released. The challenge comes when we feel it rising and we do everything in our power to distract ourselves from it, to medicate it, to push it back down. Professionally, I have learned a bit about the kind of 'freezing' of emotions that can happen when individuals are faced with extreme trauma—torture, rape, witness of violence against one's loved ones—and while the symptoms and recovery from this type of trauma can be severe and can take a prolonged period of time, I have also witnessed miraculous self-healing abilities in people who have gone through the most extreme trauma imaginable. What is happening to most of us throughout our lives with our 'mini traumas' or, in some cases, major traumas, is that we choose to ignore or push aside the emotions, and they will wait patiently for our attention.

When you are ready to be present, try sitting in silence or meditation, take a slow walk and stay focused on each step, on the breath, anything to keep you present in your body. This will help you more than any distraction you find. On the days when the flow does come more easily, when you are relaxed and energized and things seem a bit easier, be grateful and make the most of these days. Spend some time in meditation or journaling or walking and allow the momentum from your positive energy to move you forward in your day, including staying open to what happens, what occurs that you may or may not have accepted. The opportunities in the present are unlimited but we tend to shut them out because they are not what we planned for or expected. As discussed in the chapter on Acceptance, cultivate the art of enjoying the surprises, the new people or situations that occur, and you will soon find a greater sense of adventure in your life.

Let go and release the need to know exactly what is coming around the next corner and be willing to admit that you don't know all the answers. Our egos have had a field day envisioning the life, the things, the people we think we need in order to be happy. Unfortunately, our small selves, another name for our egos, know nothing of happiness and so this is where not knowing comes in. It is here in this place of not knowing that asking for 'higher guidance' comes in, and then being ready and willing to allow ourselves to be led in a new direction.

Surrendering in flow does take practice for most of us. Try sitting down with a notebook for one hour. See what happens. If you like art, get an easel and paint, and allow yourself to be inspired. If cooking is your thing, peruse through the cookbook and allow yourself to be led to a recipe that you might not have otherwise looked twice at. Be open to different ideas than you have had in the past. Your openness will allow the quiet voice inside of you to be heard. Allow yourself to be inspired and see what happens.

Another key to surrender is to let go of fear and more fully allow yourself to give and receive love. Ultimately, this is a huge part of what our human lives are all about. Yet our culture helps us get distracted so that some of us spend 90% of our day in cubicles working on projects we don't love with people we don't love for a cause we don't love. Myself included! Yet, with each passing year it becomes clearer that the key to unlocking all our joy and happiness rests with this one idea. We are here to love God, love ourselves, and love one another. And love is an action verb, meaning we can't just say we love; we must actively love. This looks different for each of us, but at its simplest: Love what you are doing at each moment and love those who are around you in each moment. This feels hard and scary, often to me as well. Most of us have been raised to think that love is hard and full of sacrifice and pain and therefore we try to control it, the same way we try to control everything else. But it does not look like what we think it looks like. It is not walking down the street, smiling at everyone you meet, although if you are called to do that, great. It is not writing love poems to the world but again, if you are called to that and enjoy it, great. Love is about surrendering control and allowing the pure, unconditional, spring of love to move through you. The more you allow this, the more you will be motivated based on the results.

Receiving love seems like it should be easy, but for many of us, this is the work of our lifetime: to find ourselves worthy enough and lovable enough to let others in to love us, and when we get hurt, not to shut down our hearts to others. We all have so many defense mechanisms that pop up consciously and unconsciously that help us to shut down our hearts, to turn inward, to stop the flow of energy between us and others. We must surrender and let go of these defense mechanisms and allow ourselves to be present, be vulnerable, and have our hearts open to receive all that others are sending to us.

How will you know when you are living a life of surrender? Your life will not be without challenges, yet you will have unshakeable faith and the feeling of being supported and guided as you encounter each day. You'll have faith that all will be well, that you are not alone, that there is nothing you can't handle. You will find life easier and more interesting as you tap into the potentials that exist in each moment. Instead of spending so much time looking backwards or looking to the future, you will find yourself living fully in today. You will be more open to journeying into the unknown as you are led beyond your self-imposed limitations and boundaries. You will find greater enjoyment in the activities you do and in the people you encounter. You will feel both more loved and more loving, which will have a positive domino effect on all aspects of your life and relationships.

QUESTIONS TO CONSIDER:

- When is a time that you are totally present and in the moment? What does this feel like?
- What is it that you love to do? Or if you can't come up with something you love to do now, what did you love to do when you were young?
- Can you remember a time when you were in flow? What did it feel like? How might you try to re-create or re-imagine that in your current life?
- What is a challenge you are currently facing? Get quiet and ask yourself: What is this challenge here to teach me? Am I willing to surrender this challenge to my Higher Self? Write down the answers.
- What would it look like for you to surrender control? To take your hands off the wheel and let your Higher Self drive? First thing in the morning, consider setting the intention: "Dear God/Universe/Highest Self, I surrender this day to you. Thank you, use me, and let's have some fun too!" And then stay loose, stay present, stay aware; the day will tell you what needs to be done!

STEP 7
CURIOSITY

"Learn from yesterday. Live for today. Hope for tomorrow. The important thing is not to stop questioning."

Albert Einstein

"Ask, and it will be given to you; seek, and you will find; knock, and it will be opened to you."

Mathew 7:7

Curiosity killed the cat? Well, perhaps but if it wasn't for curiosity our lives would be quite boring as we would just continue to do, say, and be what we have always done, said, or been. Curiosity is the fuel that drives innovation, creativity, and forward progress. "Is there a better way to do this?" "What would happen if we moved to that city?" "Why is it that I never seem to enjoy my jobs?" "What is it about this relationship that is not working for me?" "What is it about that person that I would like to emulate?" Curiosity drives questions that call forth an answer or if not an answer, a journey toward the answer. In this way, curiosity may be one of the most fundamental aspects of a healthy and purposeful life and yet, only in certain times and places—for example, teaching the scientific method—do we encourage children and even adults to ask and seek answers to high quality questions. I believe that high quality lives are created from individuals who continue to ask high quality questions throughout.

If you want to bring more clarity to your life, you must dig deeper than you have in the past. You must ask different questions and allow the answers to come. Part of why we end up repeating the same situations and feeling like we are in a rut is because we allow our actions and our thoughts to be on autopilot. While this can save needed energy in a day, week, month, or year, there is a downside to allowing yourself to get too comfortable, to become a slave to your own habits, because the changes that you wish for—inside yourself and in your environment—don't have enough room to come in if we continue to do what we have always done. Questions are a simple and powerful way to access deeper answers, better options, new pathways. Thus, if you want to find your highest wisdom, you must ask yourself questions. Not once a year on New Year's Eve and not once per month when you are working with a coach. You must do this regularly and with the expectation of answers. For many people, keeping a journal and keeping a running list of questions is helpful as they get started. In our culture, we have learned how to answer questions. We like to tell people that we know the answer. This is great for succeeding at school within the limits that are put there. But it is a terrible way to go through life. The more questions you ask, the more you will be led by your Highest Self to find the answers.

When you enter each day, do not tell the day what it will be for you. Allow the day to unfold and ask specific questions to let it show you the way. And then pay attention. Closely. The Universe will provide answers to your questions in the most amazing ways. Something you read, something someone says, a sign that resonates, a still quiet voice in your head, a letter or email that arrives... There are no limits on the ways you will see and hear the answers to your questions. Be open to these answers; these are you—your Highest, most Divine Self—giving you guidance, letting you know the way. Experiment. If you think you are guided to do something, try it and see what happens. The more you learn to trust your intuition and the signs all around you, the more you will realize you are not alone and that there is a better way to live. This realization will give you great peace. And it will give you a way of going through your day that is far more fun and enlivening than putting a task list together at the start of the day. But what about all those tasks, you ask? Ask yourself, what the best way to proceed on a particular topic is, and see what comes up. When is the best time for me to write the report? 3:00 Sunday. OK, great, so show up at your computer at 3:00 on Sunday. Or don't—you are still at choice in these matters—but recognize when you are given guidance and recognize what happens when you heed that guidance.

What type of questions should you ask? Anything. This is the fun part. Big and small, it doesn't matter. I ask questions about my purpose, the gifts I need to share more of, the future for my family and my children. I ask about which direction to go when faced with competing alternatives. I ask about the purpose of new and existing relationships, including the challenging ones. I even ask simple things like what I should wear for the day. I sometimes forget to do this, but when I remember, I always feel great about my choices. Have fun with this. It is your life and you get to ask whatever questions you want. You can ask your friends, you can ask Siri or Google, or you can ask your Highest Self—you decide who gives the best guidance!

What of extremely difficult issues—pain, anxiety, illness, death, grief? Ask about these too. Ask what is going on. Ask what you need to learn from the situation. Ask how you may be a gift in the situation. Ask what the best way to let the grief pass is. These are not easy topics and I don't mean to sound cavalier, but access your own wisdom, always and in all ways, but especially in these times. You will be amazed by the comfort you feel when you realize the support that is all around you. Of course, you may go to the doctor or a counselor or a pastor, but when you ask for guidance, you may also be guided to a specific doctor or another way to explore what is going on. Do not presume the answers.

How many questions do you ask in a day? For most of us, we spend much of each day telling what we know, sharing what we believe, and deciding what we think about something (i.e., good, bad, indifferent). When we do ask questions, it is often to solve a concrete problem we have. "Siri, how do I get to the school?" An important thing to remember: the better the questions, the better your life! So, how to cultivate the habit of asking great questions to yourself and to others? Again, not hard, just practice. Get curious. About your sensations, your feelings, your energy, your body, your interactions, your environment, other people, those you know well, those you don't know at all. A freeing thing here is that you don't have to use words to ask all the questions you want to, believe it or not, it works equally well to ask questions in your mind, even if they are to others.

Why is asking questions important? Because it opens things up instead of closing things down. It puts you into the role of learner, and there is always much to learn. With regards to the decisions we make, the small ones, and the big ones, we have a personal guidance system, our Highest Self, which knows the best decision to make at any time. To tap into this knowledge is to ask yourself honestly what to think, what to do, how to be. When you feel uncomfortable about something, ask yourself why. What is the sensation? Where is it coming from? What does it want you to learn? It may sound silly at first but try it. Try it with yourself and try it with others. You will quickly realize how much time you spend trying to tell others what to think or what to do, instead of asking them to share with you.

Questions Will Help Maximize Your Creative Potential.

After many years of coaching, I am convinced that one of the little-known secrets of success has to do with asking great questions. Asking great questions of yourself, of others, and of God. Albert Einstein is an example of someone who spent his entire life asking big questions of the universe and in turn, continued to receive information that had never been understood by humanity before. Einstein himself taught others the power of curiosity and believed this to be one of the more lasting and consequential pieces of his legacy. Unfortunately, our education system in the US and in many countries around the world fails our children not because of the content of the academics, but rather because we teach our children that there is a right answer to many questions and that they are smart if they know 'the answer' as opposed to teaching them and encouraging their natural curiosity to ask challenging questions, even those questions that do not have easy answers. Einstein has many quotes on the importance of questioning but two of them stick in my mind: **"It is a miracle that curiosity survives formal education."** He also said, **"I never teach my pupils. I only attempt to provide the conditions in which they can learn."** We become narrower and narrower as a people when we teach and believe that we already know all that can be known about life, science, math, our professions, etc. Those of us that are willing to continue to ask the questions, even those that may seem simple or silly, will benefit in our expanded minds and lives.

You may ask, "Is the power in the question or is the power in the answer?" I believe the answer is both! Questioning gets you into a space to receive. The space of asking and receiving is a high place, a place that acknowledges you don't know and that you are willing to see things and understand in a new way. Often it is only this willingness, this openness, that is lacking when things feel 'stuck'.

Keep in mind that being curious does not only mean asking lots of questions. In fact, being curious might mean you talk less and listen more. I often teach a concept in my coaching and classes for leaders called 'Listen to Learn', which at first blush sounds simple and yet this is always a challenge for most of us. Most of us: 1) listen to defend or justify our thoughts, behaviors, or beliefs, or 2) we listen to influence or persuade someone to a thought, behavior or belief. The third way to listen which we call 'listen to learn' is when the intention is to understand what the other person is trying to communicate with their words, tone, non-verbals, etc. I encourage you to try this. Try out listening to learn or to gain deeper understanding as your primary intention the next time you talk to someone. Don't think about what you will say next or how you will connect what they are saying to what you are thinking about or care about. Just be in the moment and really see what you can pick up. First, I think you will find it to be freeing in a surprising way. It is not obvious to us when we are in dialogue that we are spending a lot of energy on so many other things besides listening. So, in this way it is a lesson in mindfulness. But beyond this, I suspect you will also be amazed at what you 'pick up' that perhaps you would have missed before. There has been research to suggest that 50–90% of the meaning we get from others is non-verbal or beyond the words that are spoken. So, when you pay attention—to both what is said and what is unsaid—you will gain a much greater depth of understanding. This greater depth of understanding, of course, will provide you with more information to influence someone with or to connect to what is important to you, yet I encourage you to try to stay focused on understanding for curiosity's sake. This will help you to be more open to what is really going on instead of prematurely making assumptions and moving on. Now, for many people this may seem like a luxury of sorts to take so much time to really pay attention and hear, and yet in my experience, when we do this, it is highly productive for whatever we are discussing as well as for building trust in the relationship, which then allows communication to go faster the next time. Many clients tell me that they are surprised by how distracted they are when they try to do this. The interesting thing is that practicing this does not make one more distracted, yet it does make one more aware of what is going on in their own thoughts, which are often jumping around from topic to topic like a ping pong ball. Having clear intention to listen should help you slow down your mind and increase your concentration. Try it out and see what you find.

When it is most hard to be curious is when you are not feeling well—physically or emotionally—and yet this is one of the most productive times to do it. "Why am I so angry? Is it really anger or something else?" "Why do I feel tightness in my chest every time he walks in the room? "These are the times when it is easier to numb ourselves than to get curious. But I encourage you to try curiosity as a tool when you are angry, upset, frustrated, sad, or even if you are feeling disconnected. Ask yourself what is really going on. When I do this myself or I do this with clients, often emotion comes up quickly. What is often just below the surface of anger or upset is sadness, overwhelm or some other more subtle emotion. Then, we can ask even more productive questions: "What am I sad about exactly? How might I lift this sadness?" Ask honestly and deeply and again, wait for the answer—you will be shown. Maybe you will get a startling clear answer from your highest wisdom that shows you clearly the pattern that is within you. Perhaps it is more of a sense or nudge and yet in either case, you are closer to clarity as you release what is no longer working for you. Yet, if you don't push yourself through the discomfort—and there will be some temporarily—then you are much less likely to gain the insight you need to reduce or remove areas that are limiting you.

We are all telling the world what it should be all the time. We teach kids this in school: "What is *the* answer? You better *know* it." We take the curiosity out and this is the fuel, this is the stuff of growth. We need to get it back! The art of asking questions will change your life. Just ask Einstein, Da Vinci, or any of the others who made a life of asking great questions. Many of the successful leaders in the world today have cultivated the art of curiosity. The curious mind considers this and wonders, "Who am I asking?" In truth, you are asking God. But it doesn't matter as it is equally true to say that you are asking your Highest Self because ultimately it is the same thing. Why does it feel scary to ask questions and have an answer provided? Because we don't trust ourselves and we aren't that confident in a loving God or a benevolent Universe, for that matter. We are worried that we will be led astray! But we will not be led astray because we each have an internal radar and guidance system that will lead us down the right path. It is just that many of us have turned our guidance systems to really low and all the steps in this book will show you how to turn up the dial on your own wisdom and turn down the dial on all those conditioned voices and directives that others have given you.

Curiosity in a relationship is a tool to enable more connection and truth to flow in. Often when we are in close relationship with others—like family members, spouses, children, close friends— we feel we know them so well that we no longer ask questions about their opinions, their intentions, their dreams for the future, etc. By making assumptions that we understand these things, and being lazy not to ask them anew, we limit ourselves and we limit the relationships from growing fully. One of the greatest reasons people feel lonely, even when surrounded by others who love them, is because they do not feel fully seen for who they are. We are so busy doing things that we allow our connections to remain at a surface level. Social media is the ultimate example of this. It does end up feeling like our relationships are cheaper, of less value, more transactional than we want them to be. This is not an argument for going deep in all conversations at all times, otherwise, many of our spouses and children would run the other way; however, it is an argument for slowing down and asking more genuine questions, sharing more real dreams and views even if that feels risky. There is a great deal of interest and momentum around the power of vulnerability, including Brene Brown's work and others', and I believe it is because people are looking for an antidote to the shallowness that they feel in their relationships.

The beauty of curiosity, just like the other concepts we have been discussing, is that there is no end. You will never be perfectly curious having asked all the important questions but rather each day anew, in each new interaction, there will be opportunities to ask questions—internally to yourself and externally to others—that will bring you greater information and perspective than you had before. It is also sure to make for a more fun day!

Many people talk about the law of attraction, where energy attracts like energy, and a great way to have fun with this is to ask a question—to yourself or out loud—and wait to see what happens. If you continue to ask the question, "What is the greatest animal that ever lived?" and you use your focus, energy, and intent on this question, you will soon find articles popping up on this topic or your friends engaging in this conversation in a way that is often surprising and fun! Some have even gone as far as to say that the quality of your life is a direct relationship to the quality of the questions you ask yourself. So, do not wait to put this concept into practice. It is easy and fun and there are no wrong questions!

You will know when you have allowed more curiosity into your life when you wake up each day with greater wonder and anticipation. You will look at the situations that show up in your day with fresh eyes and you will be more present and mindful. To ask high quality questions and listen—to yourself and others—means you will be more present for each day. Questions will start to come to mind even before the assumptions and judgements come. The questions you ask and the answers you are given will lead you step by step into new and unexpected directions toward a more purposeful, adventurous, and fulfilling life.

QUESTIONS TO CONSIDER:

- How am I feeling in my body? Are there places that feel tight or painful? For each one that does, take a big breath through that part of the body. Ask *each* place of discomfort, "What do you need from me?" and then listen. You may get the answer immediately or it may come to you in some way later (could be that it pops into your mind or could be that you read something relevant or someone tells you something related) but be prepared to hear the answer.

- Consider keeping a journal with you throughout the day and writing down whatever questions come to mind. Go on about your business and when you sense the answer, pull out the journal and write it down.

- Regularly ask yourself: What gifts, talents, and potentials do I have that want to be released and shared? What is the best thing I can do with the next 30 minutes? What do I need to learn from this? Where is the light in this situation? Where is the darkness that is hard for me to look at and why? Where inside of me do I know that everything is OK? These are helpful questions that can guide you to get the most out of your day and out of a challenging situation.

- What questions do I shy away from asking because I may not want to hear the answer? How can I build daily practices that allow me to ask these questions, to feel deeply and to release what needs to be released?

CONCLUSION

7 Steps to Clarity is a path, a way forward that you must take for yourself and with yourself. While it is not a linear path, each step you take with purpose and intention will have positive consequences on you and your life. Take small steps each day: be aware, be honest, take responsibility, be courageous, accept what is, let go of the past while surrendering to the present moment, and stay curious. These small steps will bring you greater clarity which will result in big changes in your life. You will notice these changes and when you do, do not stop. Go deeper and drive greater clarity for yourself, who you are and why you are here. With that clarity will come peace, calm, confidence and a sense of joy and happiness. Share these things with others which will help them to grow and more firmly secure these traits in you. While it may take a lifetime for each of us to fully integrate these teachings, each step will bring us more freedom to be ourselves, the selves we were meant to be.

In my coaching, I have found that often when people share a struggle they are having, their perceived options for addressing the struggle are all externally focused. For example: "Should I stay at this job with this difficult boss or look for a new one when I am not sure that the setting will be any better?" A large part of my work is helping them reframe the challenge from an external one—stay or go—to an internal one: "In this situation with my current work and a difficult boss, who am I being? What do I have control over that can influence this situation (e.g., my attitude)?" Choosing to leave without really exploring our contributions to the current state, inevitably would lead to us having to learn this lesson in a new, yet similar setting. Use the 7 steps to clarity to help you to go inside, to learn the lessons now, and then you can decide where you need to take action. When you approach it in this way, often the external decision may reveal itself more clearly. It is my experience working with many hundreds of people, that as soon as we are willing to really look deeply at ourselves and our contributions to the challenge at hand, the Universe will support us in making the changes that need to be made.

Wake up to each day as if it is new and unique because it is. Partly the mundane of each day is because we bring our histories and our stories into each day with us and therefore, we separate ourselves from all that is possible. This is where our miracles are made. And they go way beyond attracting a new or better boyfriend or girlfriend or a free vacation to Hawaii. I am talking about attracting a future that you can't even believe is your life because it is so good. But that attraction is in *this* moment. So show up fully to this moment and you will know that it is working when you start to enjoy your life more as you connect with the guidance that is within you. Then do it again tomorrow! "Today is the first day of the rest of your life" is not a bad way to think about the opportunity that exists for you to fully live.

It is important to remember not to get discouraged. There is no such thing as a life without challenges, yet there is always so much more help available to you than you realize. Don't take my word for it; start to experiment. Ask questions, ask for what you think you need, ask for understanding and insight and then pay attention. The answers will come—not always in the ways you expect, but often with speed and in fascinating ways. Yes, there are lots of people that can help you with this—therapists, coaches, counselors—and while incredibly helpful for many, you ultimately don't need these people. You have all the answers within yourself.

Clarity comes when you allow it and not one minute sooner. While it can come in an instant, for most of us it comes gradually over time as we allow ourselves the moments of insight, the release of pain and worry, the gratitude about all that has been given us. With each question we ask ourselves and then receive the answer and act on the answer, we increase our trust in ourselves and our intuitions.

There is nothing wrong with distraction, entertainment, fun living, but we must stay focused on understanding ourselves better since this is work that only we can do for ourselves and by ourselves. Do not give up as each day is a new day and you will have so many opportunities to try out these steps in your own life as you open your eyes to them. The world has led us away from our natural GPS, and now it is time for you to reclaim your own highest guidance and wisdom. You *will* find greater clarity which will allow you to claim the confidence, happiness, joy, and peace that you have yet to fully claim! And then the clarity that you hold will be a gift you share to inspire many others who strive to gain their own clarity and live their best lives.

CPSIA information can be obtained
at www.ICGtesting.com
Printed in the USA
BVHW041323070423
661948BV00003B/550